PRINCIPLES
OF SPIRITUAL ACTIVISM

PRINCIPLES
OF SPIRITUAL ACTIVISM

☙

Avraham Weiss

KTAV PUBLISHING HOUSE, INC.
Hoboken, New Jersey 07030

Library of Congress Cataloging-in-Publication Data

Weiss, Avraham.
    Principles of spiritual activism / by Avraham Weiss.
    p. cm.
ISBN 0-88125-766-4
    1. Judaism and social problems. 2. Jews--Social Conditions. 3. Judaism and politics. 4.
Jews--Politics and government. I. Title.

HN40.J5 W45 2001
296.3'.6- - dc21

                                                            2001050210

Distributed by
Ktav Publishing House, Inc.
900 Jefferson Street
Hoboken, NJ 07030
201-963-9524 FAX 201-963-0102
Email orders@ktav.com
Web www.ktav.com

For my father Moshe Weiss, my first teacher of spiritual activism.

Spiritual Activism After September 11

The September 11 tragedies in New York and Washington have cast a long shadow over all of us, Jew and non-Jew alike, compelling us to reevaluate our lives in the wake of that horror. As human beings, we feel vulnerable in the face of irrational forces overflowing with hatred, unsure of what the future may bring. As Americans, we feel deeply the unprecedented violation of an enemy attack on our mainland, and the danger to our troops defending our democratic values in far off places. And as American Jews in particular we are naturally greatly concerned about the effects of this event and its aftermath on the well-being and survival of Israel.

Yet while we are now challenged with a reality that is a marked departure from anything we have confronted before, there are principles to guide us. At no point in my career have I felt more keenly the need to apply the principles of spiritual activism as when I stood day after day at Ground Zero, the site of the ruins of the World Trade Center. Here I along with other spiritual activists prayed for the peace of the thousands of souls caught in the carnage. We attended to the bereaved. We ministered to the selfless men and women struggling to repair the devastation and reaffirm the value of life.

So though things are certainly different after September 11, at heart little has changed. The principles outlined in these pages which have evolved over many years are perhaps more essential now than ever before as the new realities oblige each of us to become spiritual activists in our private lives, as citizens of the United States and the world, and as members of the Jewish community.

Contents

Introduction xi

A Parable: It's in Our Hearts xvii

Opening Reflection: A Personal Note
Family Takes Precedence Over Causes xix

I. Foundations: *Yesodot*...1

    The Partnership Between God and Humankind......................3
    Balancing Public Protest and Quiet Diplomacy 7
    Activism Is Any Action that Benefits the
    Larger Community..12

II. Pillars: *Amudim* 17

    Ahavat Yisrael—Loving Other Jews 19
    Pe'ilut Yisrael—Acting on Behalf of Other Jews................22
    Ruach Yisrael—Nurturing Jewish Spirituality 25
    Medinat Yisrael—The Centrality of the State of Israel..............28
    Achdut Yisrael—The Unity of Israel 31

III. Principles: *Ikkarim* 37

    CHOOSING THE CAUSE..38
    1. Speak Out Because It's Right,
        Not Because It's Popular 39

2. Demand for Ourselves No Less Than We Demand
    for Others 42
3. Racists Never Preach Racism Alone 46
4. Reject Collective Guilt..49
5. Go After the Big Guys..53
6. Speak Out Not Only for the Living,
    But Also for the Dead 59

MAKING PARTNERS 64
7. The Jewish Community Is a Symphony................................65
8. Rabbis Should Play a Leading Role in Activism 68
9. Orthodox, Conservative and Reform Jews
    Should Work Together 72
10. Youthful Brashness and Naiveté
    Can Have Great Impact 76
11. Older Adults Play a Crucial Role in
    Spiritual Activism 81
12. Non-Jews Can Play a Crucial Role 87
13. There Must Be Ethics in Accepting Money
    for Activism 93
14. Never Trust Leaders Who Say "Trust Us" 96
15. Activism Is Spiritually Encountering Our Fellow Jews....99

DESIGNING THE STRATEGY 102
16. Understand How Public Protest Works................................103
17. Deal Honestly with the Media...106
18. Understate the Facts 110
19. Learn the Power of Tenacity 113
20. Be There on Time..117
21. Go Into the Lion's Den 121
22. Strident Action Should Be an Instrument
    of Last Resort 124
23. Reject Violence as a Means of Social Action 129
24. Understand How to Create a Spiritual Center 133

THE HUMAN FACTOR 137
25. Never Forget the Human Factor 138
26. Everyone Can Make a Difference 141
27. With Passion the Impossible Can Be Accomplished 145
28. Learn to Cope with Fear...................................149
29. Know How to Laugh...154
30. Leadership Sometimes Requires Quiet Strength 158
31. Tame the Ego 161
32. Don't Be Seduced by Access to Power...............165
33. The Welfare of Demonstrators Takes Precedence
    Over the Cause Itself..169
34. Respect the Other..173

THE AFTERMATH 176
35. Deal with Anger and Criticism while Operating
    from the Fringe...177
36. Seek Consensus in Israel...................................181
37. Be Able to Criticize Oneself and One's Movement
    in Front of One's Own Constituents..................184
38. Every Struggle Has Its Price 187
39. Never Despair 191
40. The False Messianism of Quick Fix Solutions.................195
41. After September 11:
    Love of America Does Not Preclude Love of Israel........198

Closing Reflection: A Personal Note
Coping with Adversity 201

A Parable: It's in Our Hands......................................205

Acknowledgements 206

Introduction

Over the past thirty years I have, alongside many colleagues, students, and other dear friends, engaged in activism on behalf of the Jewish people. Beginning with the movements to free Soviet Jews and to defend the State of Israel, I have taken part in hundreds of demonstrations, marches, vigils, hunger strikes, and acts of nonviolent civil disobedience. In some of the more celebrated of these actions I have publicly confronted such notorious anti-Semites as David Duke and Louis Farrakhan, climbed over a fence and led supporters in a "sit-in" to protest the presence of a Carmelite convent at the Auschwitz death camp, and carried a coffin to the official residence of New York City mayor David Dinkins to protest his allowing police to stand back while Jews were being viciously attacked during the 1991 Crown Heights riots.

My career in activist politics began in the late 1960s as the almost instinctive and visceral reaction of a young Jew, born at the tail end of the Holocaust, to what I understood to have been the tragically wrongheaded silence of the American Jewish community during the 1930s and 1940s. As a young man, I was determined to do my part to ensure that never again would we look away and go on with our lives while our sisters and brothers elsewhere in the world were being persecuted or murdered. Yet over the decades, my efforts on behalf of the Jewish people have evolved from that heartfelt cry of "Never Again" into a philosophy of activism that is multitiered and quite complex.

"Complex" is a word that is rarely associated with activism, which is often dismissed as reflexive, nonthinking, and simplistic. A widely held view is that the activist invariably reacts quickly and with little forethought, simply holding up a sign and making a lot of noise to protest a particular issue.

Not so. Activism is precisely what most people believe it is not. It involves serious analysis, grappling with tough political issues, and attaining an understanding of the ethical precepts that must be at the heart of any planned action. For me, the thread that binds together the myriad of diverse moral, political, and tactical equations of this introspective approach to activism is Torah. Torah thoughts pervade everything, weaving a tapestry throughout the activist experience. This means that every action is based on a series of principles that are deeply spiritual in nature.

The purpose of this book is to elucidate some of those principles. This is the first of two projected volumes on activism. The second, to be written with Walter Ruby—one of the finest American Jewish newspaper writers—is a memoir of my activist career. The present book outlines the principles that helped guide these experiences.

Activism can be viewed as a kind of tree, with roots, trunk, and branches. The roots are the foundations (yesodot) upon which all else is based. The activism to which I aspire has the underlying recognition that God did not create a perfect world. From this recognition is derived the first foundation of activism: our responsibility to join God in partnership to repair this imperfect world. This responsibility is "why" we engage in activism. An understanding of "why" leads to the second foundation: the question of "how." How should we best work to carry out this repair—through public protest, quiet diplomacy, or other means? The "how" question brings us finally to the question of "what." What issues are appropriate for activism? From this question we derive the third foundation of activism: the understanding that we must not only focus on "hot" political issues touching Jews in Israel, America, and around the world, but must also commit ourselves to undertaking any action that betters the lot of human beings in need. These acts, often less glamorous but every bit as essential, include visiting the sick, tending to the dead, helping to improve the lot of the physically and mentally challenged, and bringing relief to the homeless.

Emerging from these roots is the trunk of the tree, here represented as the pillars (*amudim*) of activism. These pillars are divided into five sections or levels of awareness that an effective and morally grounded activist must attain. First, one must feel a special love for the people on whose behalf one is acting (*ahavat Yisrael*). Second, that love must be translated into action (*pe'ilut Yisrael*). Third, the ultimate goal is to bring not only physical succor to those in need, but spiritual sustenance as well (*ruach Yisrael*). Fourth, for Jews, that sustenance is inspired and guided by our special relationship to the land of Israel (*Eretz Yisrael*). Fifth, to flourish we must have a deep and abiding sense of unity (*achdut Yisrael*).

Thus, the first two and last pillars deal with the necessary ingredients to defend the people of Israel (*Am Yisrael*). The third pillar underscores the absolute necessity for the nation to have a mission; this spiritual quest is spelled out in the Torah (*Torat Yisrael*). And the fourth pillar adds the centrality of the land of Israel (*Eretz Yisrael*) in securing *Am Yisrael* physically and spiritually. It follows that the pillars underscore the fundamental elements mentioned by Rav Avraham Yitzhak HaKohen Kook, the first Ashkenazic chief rabbi of Israel, as critical to our existence—the nation of Israel, according to the Torah of Israel, in the land of Israel.

The trunk then branches out in all directions and these branches are the principles (*ikkarim*) that help to guide the activist. The essays outlining the principles are organized into five groups that build upon one another. The first group, "Choosing the Cause," consists of essays that focus on how to decide which endeavor to support on the basis of the established ideals and commitments that determine the activist's involvement. The second group, "Making Partners," emphasizes the necessity of creating alliances to achieve success once the cause has been chosen, and discusses how to determine who are appropriate partners and who are not. The third group, "Designing the Strategy," takes on the question of tactics—mapping out the fundamentals of the "how-to" of activism—once the cause and proper partners have been chosen. The fourth group, "The Human Factor," stresses the activist's need to be aware of human strengths and weaknesses, as well as the role of character in achieving success. The fifth and final group of essays, "The Aftermath," deals not only with the consequences of any activist effort, which inevitably reshape, redirect and may even give a different understanding to the cause itself, but also considers how activists often fall short of achieving total success.

Before and after the text I offer personal reflections. In the first I discuss some of the effects of my activism on my family life, and my personal quest to seek a balance between devotion to loved ones and devotion to a cause. In the final one I write about a serious personal health struggle that has affected my activism. I include this personal account in order to share with the reader a sense of the challenges that all of us must go through as we seek to help others. What also emerges from this final reflection is the importance of using our energy as positively as possible—not to allow that which we cannot do to control what we can do.

The book evolved over a period of years during which I wrote a wide array of essays for Jewish newspapers and journals throughout the United States. To be sure, many of these essays were not originally written with the purpose of spelling out activist principles. Often an essay focuses on a particular question that was pressing at the time, but from it a principle of activism can be derived that has meaning far beyond the burning issue of the moment. Several essays, although the product of thinking through the years, were written specifically for the publication of this book. Dates of the essays indicating when they were written are listed at the conclusion of each piece.

Since these essays were written over many years, I ask the reader to indulge a voice and spirit that has inevitably evolved over time. The earlier essays tend perhaps to seem more strident, narrower in scope. In contrast, those written later about struggles in which we were engaged then may seem softer, more open to alternative views. Though such a transformation is characteristic of age and experience, I am nevertheless confident that in their entirety, the essays convey a unified and coherent vision of spiritual activism. In achieving that unity of vision, I am again indebted to Rabbi Saul Berman who helped to organize the principles into the five clearly defined groupings outlined above.

Because my primary concern is with the Jewish community, the book has an overwhelmingly Jewish focus. But the principles expounded here are universal to activism and should be relevant to advocates of any just cause.

I have given the book the title *Principles of Spiritual Activism* because the term "spiritual activism" encapsulates my approach. It is hoped that the reader will glean from these essays the spiritual underpinnings so crucial in carrying out political activism in the moral and ethical realms.

There is another reason I have chosen this title. Some have argued that people help others solely out of self-interest. That is most true relative to nation-states. Regarding individuals, however, I am a firm believer in Viktor Frankl's idea that people seek meaning in life and thus help others primarily because it is the right thing to do. Perhaps the most fundamental principle in Judaism is that every person is created in the image of God. As God gives and cares, so too do we, in the spirit of *imitatio Dei*, have the natural capacity to be giving and caring. In doing so, we reflect how God works through people. The challenge to activists is to ignite the divine spark present in the human spirit and thereby impel people to do good for others. Hence the term "spiritual activism," as all action emerges from this spiritual, divine base.

It ought to be added that the term "spiritual activism" encapsulates a uniting force in all of those who do for others regardless of religious observance, commitment, or background. Also the term reminds activists who too often are caught up only in physical defense that the real goal is to find spiritual, meaning and direction in life.

The Talmud teaches that when we arrive in the next world, we will be asked a series of questions. The final question—reserved for the end, I believe, in the spirit that the very last is the most endearing—is, "Did you help redeem the world?" In other words, did each of us do our share to help repair the wrongs that plague humankind? It is my hope that this book will in some small measure help inspire such repair.

Avraham Weiss
Chanukah 5762, December 2001

A Parable: It's in Our Hearts

Once, in the kingdom of Solomon, there lived a two-headed man. Upon the death of his father, the man became embroiled in a bitter dispute with his brothers and sisters over the inheritance. "Since I have two heads," he claimed, "I deserve twice as much of the money as the rest of you." His siblings responded, "Perhaps you have two heads, but you have just one body. Therefore, you deserve only one share."

The case was brought before Solomon the king, the wisest of the wise. This is what he said: "Pour boiling water over one of the man's two heads. If the second head screams in pain, then we will know he is one person. If not, it will have been determined that the two-headed person is in fact two separate independent individuals."

So too with the Jewish people. If one in our family nation anywhere in the world is in pain—in effect, has boiling water poured over his or her head—and if we feel that pain and scream in agony even if our own heads have not been scalded, then we will have proven that we are one. If not, we will have shown that we are nothing more than a fragmented and discordant nation.

May we always feel the suffering of our fellow Jews—of all people. And may God, with infinite love, also grant us the ability to feel the dance, the song, the celebration, and the joy of our sisters and brothers.

Opening Reflection: A Personal Note

Family Takes Precedence Over Causes

Driving my daughter, Dena, to her elementary school years ago, my mind was focused on a myriad of problems facing Israel. I heard Dena mumbling something in the background but it all seemed muffled to me. Then she blurted out one word: "Rabbi." I pulled the car over. "Dena I'm your father," I said. "Why did you call me Rabbi?" Her response was one I'll never forget. "I've been calling out Abba (father) over and over and got no answer. The minute I said Rabbi, I got your attention."

No doubt many parents who are absorbed by pressing commitments can relate to this story. We are so preoccupied with everything we believe we must accomplish that we often forget those who are closest to us—our family members. In particular, activists who feel themselves obliged to respond quickly to unfolding events may experience this dilemma especially keenly.

Not only may our hearts and souls, as well as our minds, be sometimes elsewhere, our activism may also be downright hurtful or painful to those who are closest to us. I had a firsthand taste of this just before our daughter Elana's wedding more than ten years ago. I had been placed under a twenty-four-hour-a-day security watch after my life was threatened. A package containing a simulated grenade with a scrawled note was left at our front door: "Kahane's dead. You're next."

Just moments after I notified the police, our living room filled with twenty top-level cops, my old friend, Tom Lowe, who had been protecting me prior to the appearance of this particular threat, leading the way. Just then, in walked Elana who was to be married in a few days. Quickly realizing what had occurred she sat down with her head in her hands, overcome by these new developments. That was just the beginning. At her wedding, cops were all over the hall, guarding our family and our guests.

As I've grown older, I have found myself frequently reflecting on the price my activism exacted in my relationship with my family. On some level all of our children benefited greatly. I remember the joy in Dena's face as she walked through the streets of Riverdale with Natan Sharansky who was spending his first Shabbat in the United States as a guest in our home. I remember the glow in Elana's eyes as she presented an etrog and lulav to Mayor Ed Koch at a massive anti-AWACS rally at our synagogue. And I remember the night that our son, Dov, no more than seven years old, greeted our honored guest, the Soviet-Jewish refusnik, Yosef Mendelevich, before our congregation of a thousand people. Our children were always in the center of things. Seeing their father so immersed in Jewish causes, I believe, helped identify them more proudly as Jews.

But there was a downside. As close as I am to my children, my time was limited. At the Shabbat table they would have to compete with guests for their father's attention. The argument that "quality time" is at least as valuable as great quantities of time devoted to one's children, is, in my opinion, specious. Being a good parent means being there all the time-at the precise moment when your children need you, not when you have time for them slotted into your schedule, which may, in fact, be a time when they do not need or want you at all.

Throughout Jewish history some of the greatest leaders had difficulty balancing their responsibility to their community with their responsibility to their inner family. Not surprisingly, each of the patriarchs and matriarchs struggled with their children. Moses, the greatest of leaders, was not succeeded by his two sons, and in contemporary times some of the most eminent rabbinic leaders were either not blessed with children or had children who could not come to terms with their father's role.

My feelings about this immensely difficult and personal problem have evolved over time. As a younger man I always thought that my kids would understand my larger responsibilities. Maybe. But what I didn't realize was that it would be at an enormous price.

How vividly I remember sitting with Dov and explaining to him that since I was following Kurt Waldheim around the world, I would miss his elementary school graduation, as it took place on the day Pope John Paul II was receiving Waldheim at the Vatican. I just had to be there, I told Dov. Dov, who at a very young age was committed to Jewish identity and involved in Jewish activism, immediately responded, "Of course I understand, Abba, you must go."

And so I did. For years I thought that Dov had been at peace with this decision. When he was arrested with me just a few years later protesting on behalf of Soviet Jewry, the arresting officer told me that under normal circumstances he would inform a minor's parents of his arrest. "This time there's one problem," the officer said. " I'm arresting this young man's father, too." As we entered the paddy wagon, I was overwhelmed with pride as the officer added, "Rabbi, I'm Jewish and I only pray that my son will be as committed as your son, and make me as proud."

So it would never have crossed my mind that Dov would have been ambivalent about my opting to be in Rome rather than Washington Heights on the night of his graduation. But just recently, in the course of a conversation, Dov respectfully and lovingly reminded me that I was not there.

And, in fact, if I had to do it again, I would never go to Rome. As important as activism is, it's fleeting; it comes quickly and passes even more speedily. The needs of your child are deeper, more lasting. Someone else could have gone to Rome in my stead, but Dov has only one father who could have-and should have-been present at his graduation.

Rav Shlomo Carlebach said that the angels we greet at the table on Friday night are our children. And when we tell the angels to leave in peace it alludes to the prayer that when our children leave our home they should depart with a feeling of Shabbat-the feeling that their parents love them.

But children can't feel that way unless parents set aside time to send that message. Thank God, my wife Toby was always there for our children. Too often, I was not. And though I have no doubt that my children know and feel, and have been strengthened by, the limitless depths of my love for them, not being present at times, either physically or mentally, when they needed or wanted me was, I now understand, a loss that was perhaps even greater for me than it was for them.

July 2001

FOUNDATIONS: *YESODOT*

The Lord in wisdom created the earth's foundations.

(Proverbs 3:19)

The Partnership Between God and Humankind

The last word of the creation story is *la'asot*, "to do." God, in effect, tells us, "I've created the world incompletely, imperfectly, and leave it to you to finish that which I have started. In partnership we will redeem the world."

The image that has most defined my activism is that of the ship *St. Louis*.

Packed with almost one thousand Jews, the German vessel slowly made its way across the Atlantic in 1939, docking just off the coast of Florida. The ship's passengers were desperate to come ashore and be free.

It was not to be. Then U.S. president Franklin Delano Roosevelt refused to allow the passengers to disembark. In the end, the boat was forced to return to Europe, where the vast majority of those aboard met their deaths during the Holocaust.

Although the plight of the *St. Louis* was widely reported in the press, American Jewry did not do its share to help. There was a deafening silence. No Jewish organization during those dark days dared to petition the president to open the doors. And the doors weren't opened. After all, we cannot expect the president to do what we do not demand he do.

From my earliest days in the rabbinate I have heard people ask how one can believe in a God who permitted the death of the Six Million. As I grow older, this question becomes more difficult, even impossible to answer. But the story of the *St. Louis* teaches that the question is not only "Where was God?" but also "Where was humankind?" God didn't build Auschwitz; people did. And God was not responsible for the deafening silence in the free world as the devastation continued.

In fact, as has often been argued, it wasn't the enemy who broke the back of European Jewry, but the silence of those who could have done more. The persecution by the enemy could have been overcome; the silence of one's own people could not.

The idea that we must always ask ourselves if we're doing our share is steeped in Jewish sources. God created the world imperfectly for the benefit of humankind. Had the world been created totally good, there would in reality be no good, says Rav Avraham Yitzhak HaKohen Kook, the first chief rabbi of Israel, for "good" is a relative term. There is good only when evil exists. In the words of Rabbi Eliyahu Dessler, there would be no challenge in a perfect world. There would be nothing to overcome. As Rabbi Chaim Volozhin notes, without evil, one could not opt to do wrong, and since to be human means, to have freedom of choice, in a perfect world we would be stripped of our humanity.

Thus, the last word of the creation story is la'asot, "to do." God, in effect, tells us: "I've created the world incompletely, imperfectly, and leave it to you to finish that which I have started. In partnership we will redeem the world."

As much as we yearn for redemption, this theory contends, redemption also yearns for us. As much as we await the Messiah, the Messiah awaits us. As much as we search for God, God, says Rabbi Abraham Joshua Heschel, searches for us.

One of the great Chassidic masters taught the idea of partnership well: "Where is God?" asked Menahem Mendel of Kotsk. "Everywhere," replied his students. "No, my children," he responded. "God is not everywhere. He is where you let Him in."

The Torah discussion of the Exodus from Egypt, the paradigmatic event that shapes the core of our understanding of redemption, illustrates our point. Having just left Egypt, the Jewish people find themselves surrounded by the sea in front and the

Egyptians behind. Turning to Moses, they complain, "Are there no graves in Egypt, that you've taken us to die in the desert?" Moses reassures them, "The Lord will do battle for you, and you can remain silent."

In the next sentence God tells Moses, "Speak to the children of Israel and tell them to move forward." This approach to the situation on God's part is rather striking in view of Moses's prior promise that God would imminently succor His people. The bleakness of the moment is compounded when one considers that moving forward would lead the Jews directly into the churning waters of the sea.

Here, Rabbi Ahron Soloveichik notes a distinction between the terms *hatzalah* and *yeshuah*. Both terms relate to being saved. *Hatzalah*, however, invokes no action on the part of the person being saved. The person is completely passive. *Yeshuah*, in contrast, is a process whereby the recipient must do his or her share in the rescue.

When emerging as a people in Egypt, we experienced *hatzalah*. God, and God alone, took us out of Egypt, says the Haggadah that we read at the seder. As a newborn is protected by its parents, so were the newborn Jewish people protected by God. Throughout the first chapters of the Book of Exodus, the operative word is *hatzalah*.

Once out of Egypt, the Jewish people, much like a child who grows up, were expected to assume responsibilities. Mose thought *hatzalah* would continue, but God declares, no—the sea will split, but only after you do your share and try to cross on your own. Hence the sudden shift in expression from *hatzalah* to *yeshuah* as the Jews stand near the sea.

Rashi, the master commentator, makes this point about God's response, "Tell [the people] to move forward." In his words, "This is not the time for lengthy prayer." The message is clear: You have already immersed yourself in prayer. Now is the time for action. The sea does not split, says the Midrash, until the Jews try to cross on their own.

I remember my son Dov, as a small child at the seder table, asking: "Why do we have to open the door for Elijah the prophet? He gets around quickly and drinks a lot. Couldn't he squeeze through the cracks?" At the seder table we reenact the redemption from Egypt even as we stress the hope for future redemption. Appropriately, we begin the latter part of the seder experience with the welcoming of Elijah, who the prophet says will be the harbinger of the messianic period. But for the Messiah to come, says Rav Kook, we must do our share, open the door and welcome him in. Sitting on our hands is not enough.

There is a lesson here for contemporary times. Israel is under great pressure to make concessions against its best interests. Oppressed Jewry in the Soviet Union, Ethiopia, Arab countries, and elsewhere are struggling for freedom. Jonathan Pollard, a victim of a perversion of justice, is languishing in his solitary cell.

I often asked my parents where their generation was fifty years ago. Too many had too little to say. Let us bless each other today that when our children and grandchildren ask us the same question—where were you when Israel and oppressed Jewry were on the line—we will have the answer. Let us pray that we will have done our share and opened the door and let God in, and recognized that the question is not only "Where is God?" but also "Where is humankind?"

April 1989

Balancing Public Protest and Quiet Diplomacy

The horror of the Shoah taught us that we should never again depend solely on the diplomatic approach. Sometimes the more direct approach is necessary. Applied exclusively, neither technique is likely to ensure the safety of Jews in peril. Used in concert, however, the two techniques offer the hope of a more positive result.

During the past several decades, key segments of the Jewish community opposed public protest as a means of succoring oppressed Jewry.

This is not a new phenomenon. The debate concerning the efficacy of public protest goes back to biblical times, all the way back to the altercation between Jacob and Esau, brothers who clashed over who would inherit their father Isaac's blessings. In the end Jacob received the blessings, but he was advised by Rebecca, his mother, to flee for his life in order to escape his brother's wrath.

Twenty-two years after their separation, Jacob and Esau met again. That rendezvous was considered by classical commentators to be the model for the way Jews, represented by Jacob, should confront the enemy, represented in the biblical text by Esau. The Book of Genesis tells us that on eight separate occasions Jacob bowed to Esau. Some commentators suggested that Jacob's repeated bowing to his aggrieved brother was an apt illustration of how Jews should interact with non-Jews. In the words of Sforno, "Jacob's humility and obeisance stirred Esau's pity."

Others insisted that Jacob's behavior was wrong—the perfect example of how proud and dignified Jews should never act. Nachmanides (Ramban) notes in his commentary that the rabbis criticized Jacob for sending messengers to Esau with a missive beginning, "Thus says your servant Jacob." These rabbis insisted that by doing so, Jacob made himself Esau's servant. They argued that the Jews similarily took the first step leading to the loss of their independence and the destruction of the Second Temple by sending ambassadors to Rome to ask for a treaty.

The conflict within the Jewish world of that era as to how to relate to the all-powerful Romans reached its crescendo with the dispute between Rabbi Akiva and Rabbi Yohanan ben Zakkai. In the wake of the sack of Jerusalem and the burning of the Temple, a Roman leader whom Rabbi Yohanan ben Zakkai had befriended asked the rabbi his heart's desire. Rabbi Yohanan requested that the Romans allow the Jews to set up a Torah center in Yavneh, a wish that was promptly granted. Rabbi Akiva retorted that Rabbi Yohanan should have demanded much more. He should have asked for Jerusalem. To which Rabbi Yohanan responded that had he asked for everything he might well have received nothing at all.

The Talmud records that on his deathbed Rabbi Yohanan ben Zakkai advised his students to fear God as much as they feared human beings. Rav Yosef Dov Soloveitchik suggests that here the Talmud is indicating that at the end of his life Rabbi Yohanan was unsure he had made the right request of the Roman leader. Perhaps he had been too fearful of the might of Rome and ought to have relied more on God and demanded the salvation of Jerusalem.

Still, it would seem that Rabbi Yohanan ben Zakkai was vindicated by history. After all, it was his rival, Rabbi Akiva, who later supported Bar Kokhba's failed attempt to revolt against Rome and reclaim Jerusalem—an abortive rebellion that cost many hundreds of thousands of Jewish lives, forced untold thousands more to leave the land of Israel and go into exile, and extinguished the Jews' last hopes of regaining some measure of independence from the Romans.

Rabbi Shlomo Riskin and others have argued that the failure of the Bar Kokhba rebellion began a nearly two-thousand-year-long period during which many Jews concluded that the best way to deal with a powerful adversary was through diplomacy—Rabbi Yohanan ben Zakkai style—rather than confrontation as advocated by Rabbi Akiva. After all, if confrontation didn't work for Akiva, why should it work for them?

This policy had mixed results. Jews in exile were often the victims of anti-Semitic edicts and brutal pogroms. Nevertheless, Jewish literature, including the Talmud and its commentaries, Jewish poetry, Jewish philosophy, and indeed Jewish community life thrived at various times during the long night of the Diaspora.

Then came our darkest hour of all—the Shoah. Perhaps it can be argued that Jews by and large did not resist the Nazi murderers in Germany, Poland, and elsewhere in Europe because as a community we had been ingrained for so many years with the philosophy of *shtadlanut,* or appeasement. That was the only path we followed. We believed that we could best ensure our survival by doing what we had done for millennia—negotiating with our oppressors. Yes, we would take our lumps. Certainly there would be losses. But in the end we would survive.

During the Shoah, however, the fiendish oppressor was implacably bent on our destruction and impervious to negotiation. In the end, six million were annihilated, one of every three Jews in the world. The horror of the Shoah taught us that we should never again depend solely on the diplomatic approach pioneered by Rabbi Yohanan ben Zakkai. Sometimes the more direct, militant approach of Rabbi Akiva is necessary. Applied exclusively, neither technique is likely to ensure the safety of Jews in peril. Used in concert, however, the two techniques offer the hope of a more positive result.

In recent times we have witnessed the effectiveness of this two-track approach. The struggle for Soviet Jewry is the most telling example of the efficacious use of public protest to back up diplomacy. From the days of the Russian Revolution to the post-Stalin era, Jews in the West expressed concern for their Soviet brethren through diplomatic channels. Despite these efforts, thousands of Jews were murdered, Jewish leaders in the Soviet Union disappeared, and emigration was virtually non-existent. In vivid contrast, large-scale public protests triggered the massive Jewish emigration from the Soviet Union that began in 1971 (not in 1930, 1950, or 1960, when secret diplomacy prevailed) and continued into the 1980s.

Indeed, the single most powerful tool that opened the gates of the Soviet Union was the Jackson-Vanik Amendment which linked trade to the West with human rights. But why in fact was this legislation passed? Only because public protest led Washington lawmakers to realize that detente could not be achieved without large scale Jewish emigration.

What is true concerning Soviet Jewry is equally true in relation to other beleaguered Jewish communities and to other causes of concern for Jews everywhere. If we expect to help secure the safety of Jews worldwide, we need to understand that we can achieve these results only through a complementary campaign of public protest and quiet diplomacy. The former gives fuel to the latter.

Despite the impressive results achieved by this more assertive approach by world Jewry in recent decades, there are those, especially on the Orthodox right, who shy away from any form of public protest on behalf of oppressed Jews. The most extreme advocates of this position contend that God will intervene only when He wills and that it is invariably wrong for Jews to act independently of God. Others insist that public protests, such as mass demonstrations on behalf of Jews in peril, are likely to cause a severe backlash against the very Jews the demonstrations are trying to help.

Spiritual activists like myself strongly disagree with these arguments; we maintain that it is a halakhic imperative for Jews to work in partnership with God. We furthermore insist that if the Holocaust has taught us anything, it is that public protest, far from rendering the threatened community vulnerable, ensures it more protection.

It must be remembered too that there were important Orthodox rabbinic authorities who were not opposed to public protest as a means of pressure. During the height of the Soviet Jewry movement, the late Rabbi Moshe Feinstein, perhaps the greatest contemporary rabbinic legal authority, authorized the reading of his personal message of blessing to the hundreds of thousands assembled at the annual Solidarity Day in New York to speak out on behalf of oppressed Soviet Jews. And, of course, during World War II Orthodox rabbis gathered at the gates of the White House to demand that President Roosevelt intervene on behalf of European Jewry.

Living as we do in the shadow of the Holocaust, we must recognize that quiet diplomacy unsupported by public protest invariably fails. It has been amply documented that the U.S. government ducked one opportunity after another to save Jews before and during World War II, shamefully allowing political expediency and economic considerations to outweigh human concerns. Why weren't America's doors opened as the *St. Louis* sailed along the shores of this country desperately seeking a safe haven? Why weren't even the disgracefully low U.S. emigration quotas for European Jews allowed to be filled? The answer is as simple as it is painful: there was not enough public outcry, not enough direct pressure by American Jewry to persuade the U.S. government to take a stand on behalf of the desperate Jews of Europe. In those days, for the majority of Jewish leaders in the West, appeasement was the way.

Perhaps fifty years ago we did not understand the power of mass public protests. Today we do. We dare not make the same mistake. We dare not be silent again.

February 1987

Activism Is Any Action that Benefits the Larger Community

Being an activist is about much more than being involved in what some call the "big causes," those that receive the most attention in the media. The "little causes," those that touch the lives of relatively few and go largely unnoticed, are equally vital. While many in public life, in the universities, and in the clergy discuss passionately the question of which "great cause" deserves the most sustained effort, to me true activism is the realization that the greatest causes of all involve basic human needs. For the lonely recipient of relief, being helped can make a world of difference—it is the ultimate of priorities.

Speaking last year from the pulpit of our synagogue in Riverdale, Danny Heumann recalled how, following the liberation of the Soviet Jewry movement's most famous prisoner of Zion, he had asked "Sharansky is free—when will I be free?"

In August 1985, when Danny was eighteen and about to enter Syracuse University, he was in a car accident. The driver was killed and Danny was paralyzed from the chest down. For more than ten years Danny has been confined to a wheelchair.

The first months of Danny's rehabilitation were enormously difficult. Nevertheless, with tremendous physical, emotional, and spiritual fortitude, and with great help from his parents, Danny prevailed. Despite his ordeal, Danny stuck to his plan to attend

Syracuse and earned a degree in television, radio, and film management. He was the first paraplegic in the United States to walk at his college graduation using braces and crutches. As Danny put it, he wanted to be just like everybody else that day. When he went up to receive his diploma, the audience gave him a standing ovation.

About a year after Danny's accident, our son Dov became a bar mitzvah. I asked Danny if he would accept the honor of being among the seven men to be called to the Torah that morning. Danny refused.

When we discussed the matter later, Danny pointed out that there was no way for him to get up the three steps to the Torah table in his wheelchair. "The whole synagogue is built with ramps," I responded defensively, "except for the sanctuary. Besides, the Torah table is only a few inches off the floor. I would have lifted you up."

This was an offer that Danny rejected emphatically. He felt that for him, ascending to the Torah meant doing so with the fullest measure of dignity and honor that one could achieve. It was then that Danny taught me something I'll never forget.

"No, Avi," he said. "When I come to the Torah, I'll come on my own or I won't come at all."

I realized then that as open and welcoming as we had tried to make our synagogue, Danny was locked out. Clearly, our congregation had the duty to include everyone by extending the system of ramps right up to the Ark and the Torah table. Never mind that the ramps were expensive and would consume space for about thirty seats that we could easily fill on a crowded Sabbath or on the High Holy Days. The ramps had to be built.

Once they were finished, something amazing happened. More people in wheelchairs began coming. And when Danny finally came up to the Torah, there were tears of joy everywhere. We were the ones who had gained more from his wisdom than we could ever repay.

For me, Danny's insistence upon equal access was a defining moment in my understanding of the nature of true activism. It reaffirmed what I had sensed for a long time but now had been taught so powerfully: that activism consists of far more than taking part in demonstrations or speaking out on street corners.

Activism is much deeper. It is any positive action that benefits the larger community. Visiting the sick, comforting the mourner, giving relief to the hungry, alleviating the plight of an *agunah* (a woman whose husband refuses to grant her a *get*, the Jewish bill of divorce), supporting the mentally challenged, demanding that day school education be made affordable, inviting people's to one's Shabbat table, providing full accessibility to everyone—all of these and more are vital and urgent expressions of activism.

We should never forget that being an activist is about much more than being involved in what some call the "big causes," those that receive the most attention in the media. The "little causes," those that touch the lives of relatively few and go largely unnoticed, are equally vital. While many in public life, in the universities, and in the clergy discuss passionately the question of which "great cause" deserves the most sustained effort, to me true activism is the realization that the greatest causes of all involve basic human needs. For the lonely recipient of relief, being helped can make a world of difference—it is the ultimate of priorities.

For those who think that advocating for accessibility is unimportant, let it be remembered that the Holy Temple in Jerusalem too had a ramp leading up to the altar. The commentaries offer many interpretations for the presence of this ramp, but it can also be viewed as a symbol of accessibility. Not only do ramps send a message of welcome to the physically challenged, but they also say to one and all, even to those not in wheelchairs, that everyone, regardless of affiliation, health, or station in life, is welcome.

What makes a synagogue beautiful? I have heard Jews with a passion for architecture debate this question at length. Some may advocate an ultramodern structure with a skylight over the altar, while others may prefer a more traditional structure. Personally, the first thing I look for are ramps. If the synagogue is accessible, it is beautiful.

To those who disagree, who feel themselves far removed from the issue and believe it has nothing to do with them, let it be said that none of us is immune from misfortunes. As has been noted, there is no such thing as the sick and the well; there are only the sick and the not yet sick.

The need for accessibility should be especially considered by synagogues in which women can sit only in the balcony. This need should also resonate with particular force in Israel, where so many soldiers wounded in defense of the state are in wheelchairs. Ironically, in Israel even more than in the United States, synagogues are built with a profusion of steps and high podiums, without ramps and with no means of rendering them accessible.

A photograph in my office says it all. It is a picture of a man sitting in his wheelchair at the bottom of a flight of steps leading up to the entrance of a synagogue. Over its grand doors is emblazoned the sentence from the Book of Psalms: "Open the gates of righteousness for me, I will enter through them." The man sits with his back to the doors, unable to enter. We have failed him. Our task is to make sure that he can face the door and to welcome him as he makes his way in on his own. As Danny Heumann has taught us, only when he can do it on his own will he be free.

July 1997

Pillars: *Amudim*

The pillar of cloud by day, and the pillar of fire
by night,did not waver in front of the people.

(Exodus 13:22)

Ahavat Yisrael—Loving Other Jews

People often ask me why I do what I do. Why do I run to Buenos Aires after a terrorist attack? Why do I travel to Oslo to protest Arafat's peace prize? Why go here, why go there? It is because I love my people. That is the basis of my activism. My people are my family. As I love my inner family, unconditionally, as I react to their pain as if it were mine, so do I relate to my larger family, *Am Yisrael*. For me the question is not "Why go to the end of the world to help another Jew?" but rather, "How can one not go to the end of the world to help another Jew?"

In the course of a dialogue with Rabbi Steven Franklin, a Reform colleague, I remarked that I feel greater pain when coming across the name of a Jewish victim of a plane crash than that of a non-Jewish victim. During a question-and-answer session I was accused of having made a racist comment. The questioner protested that one should feel equal pain for all human beings.

Was he right? Is it racist for Jews to love other Jews more than non-Jews?

In the Torah there are two distinct commandments relating to loving one's fellow human beings. One is the *mitzvah* to love humankind, *ahavat habriyot,* since every human being is created in the image of God. The other mitzvah is related specifically to the love of one's fellow Jew, *ahavat Yisrael*. Why is there a separate Torah admonition to love Jews? Shouldn't love of Jews be subsumed under the general commandment to love everyone?

Responding to this question, Rabbi Ahron Soloveichik suggests that the two loves are fundamentally different in nature. Loving all humankind is an intellectual love. It is a love that emanates from the mind, from objective reasoning. This love is conditional. If you cease caring about me, I cease caring about you. It is a love dependent upon its being reciprocated.

Loving other Jews, on the other hand, is an emotional love. It is a love that emanates from the heart and is subjective. This love is unconditional. I love you regardless of whether you love me. If you cease loving me, I still continue loving you.

The distinction becomes clearer when one compares love of family to love of non-family. I love my spouse, children, grandchildren, parents, and siblings in a way I don't love others. My connection is emotional. The love for them is more intense.

Would anyone accuse an individual of being prejudiced because he or she feels more pain when hearing that a family member rather than a non-family member has, God forbid, been tragically struck down? Is it not natural to feel the intensity of that loss more powerfully than the loss of others outside one's innermost circle?

Am Yisrael (the People of Israel) is my family—not my inner family, but my family nonetheless, my larger family. Rabbi Judah HaLevi, the medieval poet and philosopher, takes this idea a step further. The Jewish people, he writes, can be compared to a human body. When one part hurts, the entire being is affected. So with *Am Yisrael*. All Jews are one body. When one Jew is suffering, Jews everywhere feel that suffering. And when a Jew dances and experiences joy, we all ought to feel the dance and the joy.

This does not mean that we do not feel the suffering and joy of non-Jews. Of course we do. Jews together with non-Jews are part of the greater family of humankind. But loving Jews is loving our "extended" family. To deny this disparity in our empathy with others is ultimately to deny our own human nature.

I always get concerned when people say, "You know, Rabbi, I love everyone." I invariably respond, "Fine, you love everyone, but tell me how do you love your father, your mother, your child?" It is easy to love everyone; it is far more difficult to love someone. This is so because when you love everyone, you don't have to love anyone. The test of the way one loves everyone is the way one loves someone.

Similarly, the test of how one loves all people is the way one loves one's own people. An enlightened sense of national identity, rather than being a contradiction to universal consciousness, is in fact a prerequisite for it. It is not uncommon to find that great nationalists are also great universalists. Natan Sharansky, the fearless fighter for Jewish rights in the former Soviet Union, is a great universalist. He played a key role on the Helsinki Watch Committee monitoring human rights conditions of all people living in the former Soviet Union.

A question I am often asked is why do you do what you do? Why run to Buenos Aires after a terrorist attack? Why travel to Oslo to protest Arafat's peace prize? Why go here, why go there? It is because I love my people. That is the basis of my activism. My people are my family. As I love my inner family, unconditionally, as I react to their pain as if it were mine, so I love my larger family *Am Yisrael*. For me the question is not "Why go to the end of the world to help another Jew?" but rather, "How can one not go to the end of the world to help another Jew?"

So I feel the pain of Jewish victims of plane crashes more than of non-Jewish victims. That's not racism. It is part of the human condition—to feel for all but to feel for family more.

November 1994

Pe'ilut Yisrael—Acting on Behalf of Other Jews

The cornerstone of love is the capacity to give to the loved one. One gives, and from the giving comes loving. The more one gives, the more one loves. What is true in personal relationships is also true about our love for the community of Israel. *Ahavat Yisrael* is not only the emotion of loving other Jews, but is translating that love into action, into actually doing something for *Am Yisrael*.

My mother, of blessed memory, and my father made *aliyah* (emigrated to Israel) in the late 1970s. Whenever my parents flew to New York, it was my responsibility, as their only child living there, to meet them at the airport.

One time my father called to inform me that at the last moment their arrival was moved up by twenty-four hours. Professing my deep love for my parents, I insisted nevertheless that I couldn't change my schedule on such short notice.

"You became a hotshot rabbi," my father responded, "and don't have time for your parents?" "I love you deeply," I protested, "but it's difficult to alter plans at the last moment."

I'll never forget my father's response. "Don't love me so much, just pick me up at the airport."

In his *Mikhtav M'Eliyahu* (Strive for Truth), Rabbi Eliyahu Dessler offers an understanding of love that in no small measure reflects my father's comment. While all people at times give of themselves to others and at times take from others, by and large,

22

Rabbi Dessler argues, people can be categorized as either "givers" or "takers."

Furthermore, Rabbi Dessler insists that the cornerstone of love is the capacity to give to the loved one. And, he adds, it's not necessarily the case that one first loves and from the loving comes the giving. The reverse is equally true and often even more powerful. One gives, and from the giving comes loving. The more one gives, the more one loves.

Years ago there was an extraordinarily successful program known as Marriage Encounter. One of its basic teachings was that love is not only a feeling, "it's a decision." After all, feelings change. One morning I may wake up feeling like loving my spouse, child, parent, sibling, or friend, and the next morning I may not. But if I've decided to love you—that is, if love is a decision—from the decision, from the action, the feeling may come. In fact, the real test of love is not only what I *feel* toward you but what I'm prepared to *do* for you.

The idea that love is predicated on action is crucial to understanding prayer, and, for that matter, all Jewish ritual. Prayer, said Rav Yosef Dov Soloveitchik, is the flip side of prophecy. Both involve dialogue. The only difference is who initiates the dialogue. In prophecy, God is the initiator; in prayer, it is the human being. From this perspective, prayer can be viewed as one's personal conversation with God.

If prayer is an expression of love, why should we be mandated to pray? Why not pray only when we feel like praying? Rabbi Abraham Joshua Heschel argues that we may not feel like praying for long periods of time. But if we're obligated to pray—if, indeed, we make a decision to pray—from placing ourselves in a prayerful mode, feelings of prayer may surface. This, in fact, is the basic idea of ritual, religious observance, which connects us to God. Perform the ritual and from the act the feeling may come. Hence Jews at Sinai first proclaimed, "We will do." Only afterward did they say, "We will listen."

What is true in personal relationships in regard to love of others and of God is also true about our love for the community.

Ahavat Yisrael is not only the emotion of loving other Jews, members of our larger family, but is translating that love into action, into actually doing something for *Am Yisrael*. It's not enough to love Soviet Jewry or Ethiopian Jewry or to feel that something must be done for Jonathan Pollard or the Israeli MIAs or for Argentine Jewry. What's necessary is to act on their behalf. While not underestimating the emotion of feeling for others, the real test is what we are prepared to do for others.

From this perspective, I have more respect for someone who disagrees with me and therefore doesn't act than for someone who agrees but for a variety of reasons doesn't act. You know the rationalizations as well as I do. I call it the "but" syndrome. In the High Holiday service it's the phrase "but (aval) we sinned," which Maimonides considers the central part of the confession. Of course I care, "but" I don't have time; I care, "but" what difference can I make? I care, "but" if I speak out my job will be in jeopardy; I care, "but" I know someone else will do it. Indifference, an unwillingness to become involved, is a greater sin than taking the wrong position.

Not coincidentally, the root of *ahavah*, love, is the two letter Aramaic word *hav*, to give. It's nothing less than what my Abba said: "Don't love me so much, just pick me up at the airport."

January 1996

Ruach Yisrael—Nurturing Jewish Spirituality

The activist grounded exclusively in physical defense—demonstrations, rallies, protests, political lobbying—doesn't understand the true nature, essence, and higher purpose of activism. If I am a Jew only to fight anti-Semitism, that is negative Judaism. If, however, I am a Jew because I appreciate the Sabbath, I treasure the Jewish laws of business ethics and all the laws and rituals that ennoble the life of the Jew, and I devote time to reading Jewish books and Torah study—that is positive Judaism.

The proliferation of well-funded organizations dedicated to Jewish defense would lead us to believe that the central challenge facing American Jewry today is anti-Semitism.

Not so. At far greater risk is the soul, not the body of American Jewry. To be sure, a soul without a body cannot function in this world; but a body without a soul is a body without direction, purpose, or meaning.

Of course there are pockets of anti-Semitism in the United States that must be confronted head on, whether it's a White David Duke or a Black Louis Farrakhan. But we should recognize that anti-Semitism is not omnipresent here. The spiraling intermarriage rate among American Jews proves this point. Throughout Jewish history, whenever anti-Semitism prevailed, the marriage of non-Jews to Jews was *verboten*. In America today, it has been pointed out, we are so free that non-Jews are marrying us in droves.

The late Professor Eliezer Berkovits was correct when he said that from a sociological perspective, a Jew is one whose grandchildren are Jewish. The painful reality is that large numbers of the grandchildren of today's American Jews will not be Jewish.

What is needed is a refocusing of our priorities. This can be accomplished by transforming our concept of Jewish defense into an expression of Jewish spirituality. When we defend Jews under attack, we should do so not only as Americans demanding equal rights, but as Jews who feel a deep bond with those in our community who are in jeopardy.

To be sure, as Jews living in America, we reject any attempt by anyone to treat us as second-class citizens. Thus, in response to Pat Buchanan's accusation that I am biased toward Jonathan Pollard because of my Jewishness, I replied in blunt terms: "I am defending Jonathan Pollard as an American. I am not asking that Jonathan be treated any better than other Americans, but I will not allow him to be treated any worse."

But while we speak as Americans, we above all we raise our voices as Jews who feel a unique connection, an emotional connection, to our people—yes, to our larger family. It is what Natan Sharansky, from the dungeons of Chistopol, described as the "unity of souls." While alone, he always felt an inextricable link to Jews everywhere.

Our first task, then, is to teach and act out Jewish defense as one of the most fundamental principles of Jewish spirituality—*ahavat Yisrael*—the infinite and endless love of all Jews.

The second task is to recognize that the essence of activism is to ignite a Jewish spark. The activist who is grounded exclusively in physical defense—demonstrations, rallies, protests, political lobbying—doesn't understand the true nature, essence, and higher purpose of activism. If I am a Jew only to fight anti-Semitism, that is negative Judaism. If, however, I am a Jew because I appreciate the Sabbath, I treasure the Jewish laws of business ethics and all the laws and rituals that ennoble the life of the Jew, and I devote time to reading Jewish books and Torah study—that is positive Judaism.

Indeed, Jewish knowledge and education constitute another pillar, Yediat Yisrael, which is inextricably bound up with the pillar of Ruach Yisrael, the spirit of Israel. Yediat Yisrael is crucial to Jewish identity, Jewish activism, and Jewish survival. In its absence, Jews are in danger of forgetting who they are, of ceasing to stand up for Jewish causes, and of casting away Jewish values and rituals, which will become meaningless through a lack of learning and understanding, and lead to assimilation and loss. Jewish knowledge, Yediat Yisrael, and Jewish spirit, Ruach Yisrael, are twin pillars which, together, encapsulate positive Judaism.

From this perspective, activist organizations must see the defense of the Jewish people as a point of entry to a greater sense of Jewish spirituality and Jewish learning. Standing up for Jews should not be the last step in one's commitment to *Am Yisrael*, but rather the first step toward rekindling greater ties to our people and inspiring greater commitment to Jewish observance and study.

Yet if we were to add up all the monies allocated for Jewish education and Jewish spirituality in one column and all the monies targeted for Jewish defense in the other, the former sum would pale in comparison to the latter. Unfortunately, in our day we are trying to fight massive assimilation with a slingshot. What is required to touch Jewish souls is a radical reprioritization of communal resources and funding. More funding is crucial in order to create, sustain, and enhance programs that foster the Jewish spirit and to attract the best leaders to the rabbinate and other Jewish professional services.

Make no mistake. The Jewish community must continue to confront anti-Semitism wherever and whenever it rears its ugly head. Yet, while the combating of anti-Semitism is an important objective in and of itself, that effort must be part of a far larger goal: the stirring and reawakening of Jewish consciousness.

June 1994

Medinat Yisrael—The Centrality of the State of Israel

But most important, the goal of the Jewish spiritual activist is to do his or her share to redeem the world. This is our mission as the chosen people and this can be accomplished only through committing ourselves to the chosen land— Israel.

It is not coincidental that worldwide Jewish activism began in earnest soon after the Six Day War in 1967. The lightning victory of the Israeli army gave Jews everywhere the courage to stand up and defend themselves.

And it is not only that Israel has inspired Jews everywhere to self-defense. The Jewish state is also the physical insurance policy for all Jews. Unlike during the Holocaust, when Jews had nowhere to flee, today we know that if anything catastrophic occurs in our country of residence, we have a place to go. This in fact is the *raison d'être* of Israel's law of return introduced just a few years after the Shoah, which grants any Jew immediate citizenship upon arriving in Israel.

The existence of Israel is also a powerful impetus to Jewish spiritual activism throughout the world. The ultimate goal of Jewish spiritual activism is to inspire greater Jewish identity and consciousness, a goal that is more difficult to achieve in the Diaspora. In connecting with Israel—the place that is at the very center of Jewish destiny—a greater sense of Jewish spirituality is fostered.

But most important, the goal of the Jewish spiritual activist is to do his or her share to redeem the world. This is our mission as the chosen people and this can be accomplished only through committing ourselves to the chosen land—Israel.

To be sure, there are those who understand the concept of the chosen people differently. They say that chosenness means the Jewish soul is superior to the non-Jewish soul. This, in turn, has created the false impression that non-Jews are less important, less valuable than Jews. Nevertheless, the mainstream approach in Jewish belief has always been based on the principle that every person is created in the image of God. The Jewish soul is not superior to the non-Jewish soul.

In fact, the first eleven chapters of the Torah are universal. God chose humankind over all species He created. But humankind did not fulfill the chosen role God had assigned to it. The world was destroyed by flood, and soon after all of humanity was spread across the earth in the generation of dispersion.

God then chose Abraham and Sarah to be the father and mother of the Jewish people. Their mandate was not to be insular but to be a blessing for the entire world. It is not that the souls of Abraham and Sarah were superior; it is rather their task which had a higher purpose.

Ultimately, we became a people who are charged to follow *halakhah*, the pathway to Torah ethicism, which leads to the redemption of the Jewish people, through which the world is to be redeemed. Our task is to function as the catalyst in the generation of the redeemed world. The movement of chosenness is not from the particular to the more particular, but rather from the particular to the more universal. Chosenness is, therefore, not a statement of superiority but of responsibility.

Of course, those who wish to join the Jewish covenantal community are welcome. And there is nothing that precludes those who are outside of the Jewish family from personally reaching the highest levels of spirituality. Quite the contrary; if we believe that they could not reach these levels of spirituality, as Rabbi Judah HaLevi states, our mission would be impossible to achieve.

The idea of our chosenness has always been associated with our sovereignty over the chosen land. From this perspective, Israel is important not only as the place that guarantees political refuge; not only as the place where more *mitzvot* (commandments) can be performed than any other; and not only the place where—given the high rate of assimilation and intermarriage in the exile—our continuation as a Jewish nation is assured. But first and foremost, Israel is the place, the only place, where we have the potential to carry out and fulfill our mandate as the chosen people. In exile, we are not in control of our destiny; we cannot create the ideal society Torah envisions. Only in a Jewish state do we have the political sovereignty and judicial autonomy that we need to be the *or la-goyim* (light unto the nations) and to establish a just society from which other nations can learn the basic ethical ideals of Torah.

Of course, Jews living in the Diaspora can make significant individual contributions to the betterment of the world. And there are model Diaspora communities that impact powerfully on *Am Yisrael* and humankind. But I would insist that the destiny of the Jewish people—that is, the place where we as a nation can realize the divine mandate to Abraham of "in you will be blessed all the peoples of the earth"—can only be played out in the land of Israel.

From this perspective, those living in the chosen land have the greater potential to more fully participate in carrying out the chosen people idea. Only there do we, as a nation, have the possibility to help repair the world—the ultimate challenge of the Jewish spiritual activist.

December 1994

Achdut Yisrael—The Unity of Israel

In international struggles the rules of protest can sometimes be harsh. Yet for me there has always been a clear difference between fighting an external enemy and disagreements within the Jewish community. In the internal disputes, we are in effect disagreeing with members of our own family. The rules therefore must be far more benevolent, based firmly on principles of love, acceptance, and loyalty.

Throughout my adult years I have fought vigorously against the enemies of the Jewish people. In these international struggles the rules can sometimes be harsh. Yet for me there has always been a clear difference between fighting an external enemy and disagreements within the Jewish community. In the internal disputes, we are in effect disagreeing with members of our own family. The rules therefore must be far more benevolent, based firmly on principles of love, acceptance, and loyalty. The idea of family and the rules that govern family relations are, I believe, at the heart of Jewish unity (*achdut Yisrael*). Jewish unity, in essence, is a family matter.

My understanding of Jewish unity has been inspired by the writings of two of the most important Jewish religious thinkers of our century, Rav Avraham Yitzhak HaKohen Kook and Rav Yosef Dov Soloveitchik. It is from their discussions of covenant (*Brit*) that I have developed my ideas about *achdut Yisrael*.

Rav Kook, the first chief Ashkenazic rabbi of Israel, describes two covenants. The first is called *Brit Avot*. Here, at God's behest,

Abraham and later Sarah are chosen as the father and mother of the Jewish people. The *Brit* is based on the family model. If you are born into the family, you are one of its members. You are, in short, part of the Jewish people.

Rav Soloveitchik, the greatest luminary of Modern Orthodoxy, speaks of a similar *Brit*, which he calls the "covenant of fate." All Jews, according to Rav Soloveitchik, share absolute commonality. We share a common history, a common sense of suffering when one of us is hurt, and a common responsibility to intervene when a brother or sister is in need.

Rav Kook calls the second covenant *Brit Sinai*. In this covenant, which took place at Sinai, we became a nation defined by a religious mission. While *Brit Avot* requires no action because one is simply born into the family, *Brit Sinai* is based on commitment to what was given at Sinai. *Brit Avot* is inborn; in *Brit Sinai* one may choose to keep or reject the commandments.

Rav Kook's *Brit Sinai* is paralleled in Rav Soloveitchik's thinking through what he calls the "covenant of destiny." This covenant is bestowed at Sinai, where we were given the mission to redeem the Jewish people, through whom in turn the world will be redeemed.

It seems to me that with respect to this second covenant—what Rav Kook calls Sinai and Rav Soloveitchik calls destiny—striking and painful differences have emerged among the Jewish people. This century has witnessed the growth of movements within the Jewish community that understand our mission in radically different ways.

There is a temptation on the part of those who promote *achdut Yisrael* to gloss over such differences for the sake of peace. That is a mistake. There are, in truth, glaring divisions within our family. For example, as an Orthodox rabbi, I do not view Reform and Conservative Judaism to be correct on such fundamental issues as *Torah m'Sinai* (Divine Revelation) and *halakhah* (Jewish Law). I especially take issue with American Reform's position on patrilineal descent—as does the Conservative movement and the Israeli wing of the Reform movement—which, I am convinced, threatens to divide our nation, our family. And indeed, Conservative and Reform rabbis do not view Orthodoxy as correct in many areas.

Still, such disagreements ought not to stand in the way of *achdut Yisrael*. Rav Kook writes: "The sanctity of chosenness (*Brit Avot*) is eternal. It is greater and holier than the portion that is dependent on choice (*Brit Sinai*)." While Rav Kook was a deeply religious and observant Jew whose commitment to *mitzvot*, the Sinaitic covenant, was central to his being, what ultimately defines the Jew for him is being part of the family. Family supersedes ideology.

Similarly, in Rav Soloveitchik's terms, argument over mission and practice must be debated within the framework of a shared fate and shared community. Those with whom we disagree should not be viewed as the enemy, as individuals who are not part of our family.

In short, while we dare not make light of our differences, even more important is that when we argue among ourselves, we do so as a family. We must be *machmir*—absolutely uncompromising—on the *mitzvah* of *ahavat Yisrael*, love of our fellow Jew. In order for us to achieve this while staying true to our individual principles, an ethics of dissent should be drafted:

- Language must be used with care. While a word is a word and a deed is a deed, words lead to deeds.
- Dissent is acceptable, delegitimization is not. No purpose is served in invalidating the other.
- No matter the extent of one's disagreement with Israel, *ahavat Yisrael* requires total material and spiritual commitment to the State, which must remain unconditional.
- Each movement should recognize that it has no monopoly on passionately loving the people, Torah, and the land of Israel.
- While disagreeing, we can learn from each other. The Orthodox can learn the universalistic agenda of *tikkun olam* (repairing the world) from the non-Orthodox, and the non-Orthodox can learn the importance of ritual and day school education from the Orthodox.

- Energy should be expended not on castigating other movements, but rather on reaching the majority of American Jews
who are unaffiliated and whose greater involvement in
Judaism must be our central focus.

In this spirit, there is one final principle that must be emphasized. According to the kabbalist, God, in order to make room for
humankind, needed to step back. This withdrawing and contract-
ing is known as *tzimtzum*. We, created in the image of God, must
do the same. As God limited himself to make room for the world,
so must we limit ourselves to make room for others. Strength is
commonly associated with acquisition of power, but in Judaism,
strength can be derived equally from stepping back and making
room for the other.

For me this means, for example, that Orthodox women's
prayer groups, which I have strongly advocated, should refrain
from praying at the present *Kotel* (Western Wall) where the
Haredim assemble for *tefillah* (prayer). Another spot along the
southern wall for such prayer must be found in order to demonstrate sensitivity to our *Haredi* brothers and sisters. In a similar
vein, as unconscionable as are the attacks near the *Kotel* against my
Conservative and Reform coreligionists, they too, in the spirit of
tzimtzum, should find an alternative spot along the southern wall
of the *Kotel* to *daven*.

As an Orthodox rabbi, I take the message of *tzimtzum* to its
fullest. For me this means rethinking the religion-state relationship
in Israel, which includes the role of Conservative and Reform rabbis there. At the very least, the reported compromise reached by
the Ne'eman commission ought to be adopted. This compromise
would allow Conservative and Reform rabbis to participate in
wedding ceremonies and in the conversion process, while leaving
the halakhic aspects of these rites to the Orthodox rabbinate.

Such a compromise requires yielding on both sides. The
Orthodox would be giving "standing" to the Conservative and
Reform rabbinate. The Conservative and Reform would be allow-
ing the Orthodox rabbinate to be the halakhic arbiters. But through

this yielding process, the unity of *Am Yisrael* would be preserved. There would be one standard for who is a Jew.

Although *tzimtzum* is primarily about making space for the other, ironically it often results in a strengthening of self. Thus, paradoxically, by making room for the other, each of the three movements, Conservative, Orthodox, and Reform, are likely to be strengthened. Spiritual growth comes through choice, not force.

So serious is the schism within our family that it poses a threat to the very survival of the State. Chosenness means, in part, that God promised that a faithful remnant of Jews would always be worthy to remain in Israel. It doesn't mean that in every generation the Jews as a people would be sovereign in a Jewish state. Whether we remain sovereign depends on us.

Most crucial to the survival of the State is *ahavat Yisrael*, loving our fellow Jews. Perhaps the most important teaching of my rabbinate has been that *Am Yisrael* must be viewed as a large family. *Achdut Yisrael* within this family is based on love. And the test of family love is how we love, even when we disagree.

April 1998

Principles: *Ikkarim*

Principle: A term applying to a concept upon which other concepts are entirely dependent, so much so that they cannot exist without the original concept.

(Book of Principles by Joseph Albo 1:3)

CHOOSING THE CAUSE

The Spiritual Activist chooses a cause because it is right.

The Spiritual Activist never feels self-conscious about demonstrating in support of his or her own rights.

The Spiritual Activist raises a voice even against a racist who might also have done some good things.

The Spiritual Activist is careful to target the precise subject of protest, rejecting collective punishment.

The Spiritual Activist is prepared to criticize the most powerful, and to speak out not only for the living but also for the dead.

Principle One

Speak Out Because It's Right, Not Because It's Popular

Almost all people are prepared to join a campaign they know they are going to win. The true activist jumps in even when victory is uncertain. It is easy to be out there with everyone else. The question is whether one is prepared to be there first, even if that means standing with few allies.

"Activist" is an overused word. It seems as if everyone today—from Hadassah women to ADL supporters to street protesters—is being referred to as an activist.

An activist is one who becomes involved in an issue not because it is popular but because it is right. Almost all people are prepared to join a campaign they know they are going to win. The true activist jumps in even when victory is uncertain. It is easy to be out there with everyone else. The question is whether one is prepared to be there first, even if that means standing with few allies.

Consider two of the great activist triumphs of recent years: the Soviet and Ethiopian Jewry movements. Who can forget that cold day in Washington in 1987 when hundreds of thousands came to speak out on behalf of our brothers and sisters behind the Iron Curtain? Equally memorable was the Friday night in May 1991 when the Israeli government airlifted thousands of Ethiopian Jews to safety in Operation Solomon.

But these two movements, while representing two of the greatest achievements in recent Jewish history, waged a tough battle just to be recognized by the Jewish powers that be. For years those who campaigned for Soviet and Ethiopian Jewry stood alone. The Jewish establishment, and even the government of Israel, marginalized, ignored, and, tragically, often worked against the pioneers of these movements.

Some examples: The Jackson-Vanik Amendment of 1974, linking trade with the Soviets to freedom of emigration, was the most important law facilitating the ultimate freedom of Soviet Jews. In the days before it was passed, three of the most influential members of the Jewish establishment asked Senator Jackson to withdraw the amendment, fearful that its passage would create a backlash among American farmers whose wheat sales to the Soviets would have been curtailed. Jackson, thankfully, did not bend.

A second example of this type of opposition occurred at the Jewish Student Network convention in Washington, D.C., in 1979. There, Ezer Weizman, then Israeli defense minister, was asked publicly what Israel was doing about Ethiopian Jews. His response to the convention, on behalf of the Israeli government, was, "Falasha, shmalasha."

Of course this disturbing phenomenon is not confined to American Jewish life. It pervades the larger American social and political landscapes. It took years before the import of the civil rights and antiwar movements were widely acknowledged. For a long time, movement leaders were reviled; they too stood alone.

So too in the biblical narrative. After Moses and Aaron persuaded the Jewish elders to join them in marching on Pharaoh's palace to demand that he "let my people go," they arrived at the palace alone. Where were the elders? Rashi, the classic biblical commentator, suggests: "One by one they dropped out until only Moses and Aaron drew close to the palace. Fearful of confronting the king, the elders were nowhere to be seen."

The Torah recognizes that the great struggles invariably begin on the margins. Abraham, the first Jew, is called *Ivri*, which means "of one side." "All the world was on one side of the river," says the Midrash. "Abraham, alone, was on the other." Still he persevered.

In contemporary times as well, it is so often the *amcha*, those from the grassroots, who generally possess the instincts, the will, the fearlessness, the sense of justice, the independence, to correctly assess the situation and understand—long before the establishment—what actions must be taken. The establishment, indeed, often rejects the means adopted by the grassroots. Despite their good intentions, the organized community is often mired in bureacratic red tape, leading them to become estranged from the amcha, and to lose their sense of vision and ability to take risks.

It has been this way not only with regard to Soviet and Ethiopian Jewry, and for that matter Syrian Jewry, but also with regard to many other issues, from the battle to demand justice for Yankele Rosenbaum to the struggle over the Auschwitz convent to the Jonathan Pollard case, to mention just a few of the better-known causes. The grassroots leads the way and, once the "coast is clear" and the issue has acquired a measure of respectability, the establishment "boldly" steps in, making sure to distance itself from and discredit those who were the first to stir the conscience of the community.

To be sure, Soviet Jewry would not be free today had there been no worldwide struggle, and Ethiopian Jewry would still be in Ethiopia had Israel not decided to airlift them to freedom. But the success of these movements should not blind the establishment from the realization that the true heroes are people like Glenn Richter and Graenum Berger, tireless fighters for Soviet and Ethiopian Jewry, who were there from the beginning. They succeeded in moving the issues from the periphery to the center, forcing the establishment and the government of Israel to confront them head-on.

So who is the true activist? One who speaks out because it is the correct thing to do. The campaigns for Soviet and Ethiopian Jews should inspire Jews the world over not to be afraid to get involved on the ground level in the physical and spiritual challenges facing the Jewish people.

December 1994

Principle Two

Demand for Ourselves No Less Than We Demand for Others

Speaking out for others carries relatively little risk and, moreover, brings the acclaim and approval of the larger community. But speaking out with equal intensity on behalf of our own interests touches upon our insecurities and heightened sensitivity to what others may think of us— insecurities and sensitivities that we, as Diaspora Jews, have acquired and absorbed over the years.

As a Jewish activist, I am passionately involved in the issues that confront our people and shape the contemporary Jewish scene.

As a human rights activist, I have a concern that also extends to promoting the well-being of other communities, whether by going to the Bronx public schools to teach that racism and anti-Semitism are essentially variations of a single theme—prejudice— or by establishing synagogue based programs for the elderly and developmentally disabled of all races, or by organizing food and clothing drives to assist the poor and hungry.

In my concern for the larger world, my brand of activism echoes the universalist agenda of traditional liberal ideology. My involvement with the welfare of all people may not be immediately apparent, because of a strong primary commitment to issues facing the Jewish people, but in writing, speeches, and action, it's always there.

Where I differ from the traditional liberal ideology is not in humanitarian concerns but in an unwillingness to give a lesser priority to Jewish concerns. My guiding principle has always been that, as Jews, we should demand no less for ourselves than we demand for others. It's a principle that too many in Jewish leadership violate.

Consider, for example, the June 1990 protest in which I was involved against the New York City ticker tape parade honoring Nelson Mandela. I am, and always have been, one with the struggle against apartheid. But Mandela had compared Israel to South Africa's apartheid government and had embraced Arafat, Khaddafi, and Castro. My message was clear: "Apartheid, no, but if you compare South Africa to Israel and embrace Arafat, you bring shame to the anti-apartheid struggle."

Jewish leaders who were in the forefront of the Mandela parade roundly condemned our actions. But what would their reaction have been had Natan Sharansky, following his release from the Soviet gulag, embraced the president of South Africa, applauding his apartheid government?

Now imagine further that soon after making such a statement, Sharansky came to New York, and the then mayor of the city, Ed Koch, a champion of Soviet Jewry, announced a ticker tape parade for him. How would our community have reacted? There is no doubt that in such a case we would have joined our Black brothers and sisters in vigorous protest. Our message, in this hypothetical instance, would have been simple: You may have been a hero, but your embrace of apartheid brings shame to the Soviet Jewish struggle.

Why would Jews have likely protested Sharansky's hypothetical embrace of apartheid but remain silent in the face of Mandela's embrace of Arafat? In other words, why do we tend to hold back and tolerate a non-Jewish public figure, however noble, who trespassed on an ethical or humanitarian principle that directly affects us and our destiny?

The readiness of Jews to protest apartheid while remaining reticent when the well-being of their own people was at stake is, unfortunately, not hypothetical. Many Jews who nobly engaged in peaceful arrest at the South African embassy protesting apartheid refused to be arrested at Soviet embassies in demonstrations for Soviet Jewry. And many Jews who were commendably in the forefront of the battle to impose U.S. economic sanctions against the South African apartheid regime were reluctant to support similar sanctions against the Soviet Union in the form of the Jackson-Vanik Amendment, which linked U.S. trade with the Soviet Union to the emigration of Soviet Jews.

Another example of how we tend to support non-Jewish concerns more vigorously than our own: I joined in opposing Rabbi Meir Kahane's plan to transfer Arabs out of Israel. But I also oppose the present peace process when, in effect, it seeks to force the transfer of Jews out of Judea and Samaria by calling for Israeli troop withdrawal from those areas, replacing them with Palestinian police and leaving Jews unprotected.

Why does that plan not inspire an outrage similar to the one evoked by Kahane's plan? Why is Arab transfer *verboten* while Jewish transfer—the Kahane plan in reverse—is sanctioned?

The answer lies in centuries of conditioning in the Diaspora. Speaking out for others carries relatively little risk and, moreover, brings the acclaim and approval of the larger community. But speaking out with equal intensity on behalf of our own interests touches upon our insecurities and heightened sensitivity to what others may think of us—insecurities and sensitivities that we, as Diaspora Jews, have acquired and absorbed over the years.

When fighting for others we feel strong and unhampered. When fighting for ourselves, though, we are deferential and afraid.

A few weeks before the Mandela parade, I took part in a panel discussion sponsored by the New York Board of Rabbis. After declaring my group's intention to demonstrate, a fellow panelist, one of the leading rabbinic figures in New York, turned to me and said: "What are you doing, Avi? You may be right in your outrage against Mandela, but this protest will turn Blacks against us." My response was that our peaceful protest will gain the respect of the Black community. If you show no self-respect, no one will respect you.

As Jews, we have a responsibility to be both universalists and particularists. While my activism is one that shares the universalist agenda, it can never be at the expense of commitment to my own people.

As Hillel said, "If I am only for myself, what am I worth?" Too often we forget that his question was preceded by and derived from an even more important one: "If I am not for myself, who will be for me?"

April 1995

Principle Three

Racists Never Preach Racism Alone

Racists never preach racism alone. They understand that people are fundamentally good and will not buy a purely bigoted message. In order to market their hate, racists consistently interlace their bigotry with positive programs. The truth is, as Professor Alan Dershowitz has argued, when bigots preach a positive agenda alongside general hatred, they become more dangerous. The good they espouse lends credibility to their racist messages.

Jack Kemp has done it again. Three weeks after praising Reverend Louis Farrakhan, leader of the Nation of Islam, the Republican vice presidential candidate in an interview with David Frost lauded Farrakhan again, insisting that "part of the message has to be admired."

Farrakhan, of course, is the bigot who has referred to Judaism as a "gutter religion," called Jews "bloodsuckers," blamed Jews for running the slave trade, insisted that Jews were responsible for the crucifixion of Jesus, and even referred to Adolf Hitler as "a great man." Most recently, Farrakhan was the honored guest of Libyan dictator Muammar Khaddafi. Were it not for U.S. law, Farrakhan would have accepted one billion dollars from the Libyan leader to aid the Nation of Islam.

Although Kemp did publicly ask Farrakhan to disavow his anti-Semitism, Kemp's support of any part of Farrakhan's program is disturbing.

Racists never preach racism alone. They understand that people are fundamentally good and will not buy a purely bigoted message. In order to market their hate, racists consistently interlace their bigotry with positive programs.

Consider Hitler, the ultimate racist, who preached hatred of Jews while simultaneously calling for the rebuilding of the German economy and pride in the German past. Should Hitler have been applauded for the good he was espousing?

Or consider the Ku Klux Klan. Their message went beyond anti-Black and anti-Jewish hate. In the 1950s they pounded home the importance of white Protestant economic power and the notion that Whites ought to take greater pride in their past. Should the KKK have been supported for the "positive" message it preached?

Of course, support of organizations and public figures does not imply 100 percent endorsement of everything for which they stand. But when they espouse anti-Semitism, we should not endorse these groups or individuals at all.

The truth is, as Professor Alan Dershowitz has argued, when bigots preach a positive agenda alongside general hatred, they become more dangerous. The good they espouse lends credibility to their racist messages. For this reason Mussolini was disavowed despite his talent for making the trains run on time. Similarly, David Duke was repudiated notwithstanding his economic program to strengthen Whites in the South. Their overall message of hate made it impossible for anyone of moral conscience to support anything they proposed. We must do the same with Louis Farrakhan. We must not praise any of his positive messages because of the racism and anti-Semitism he simultaneously proclaims.

In protesting against anti-Semitism and bigotry, we do not discriminate. Racism and anti-Semitism know no particular nation, color, or religion. There are White racists and anti-Semites like David Duke, and Black racists and anti-Semites like Louis Farrakhan.

I purposefully refer to Duke and Farrakhan as racists and anti-Semites because Duke is not only anti-Jewish but anti-Black even as Farrakhan is not only anti-Jewish but anti-White. Duke and Farrakhan are living proof that racists are anti-Semites and anti-Semites are racists.

As we protest against Louis Farrakhan, however, we of course will not allow his bigotry to turn us against African-Americans. In fact, some African-American leaders have taken the positive step of repudiating Farrakhan, and many did not attend his most recent rally in New York. The test of leaders is their willingness to criticize not only others but also members of their own constituency—to their face when necessary.

Jack Kemp and others of good will should understand that it is simple to speak out against bigotry when a bigot has little positive to offer. The challenge is to raise a voice of strong protest even when the bigot's message is mingled with positive programs. The vice presidential candidate may be speaking softly about Farrakhan in an attempt to curry favor with some African-American voters. The price is too great to pay when, in the process, the anti-Semitism preached by Farrakhan gains credibility through such an endorsement.

February 1996

Principle Four

Reject Collective Guilt

We dare not allow the evil of one man, of one group, to turn us against an entire race. Rather, we must peacefully confront those individuals and only those individuals, those groups and only those groups, who are racist and anti-Semitic.

"You see everybody always talk about Hitler exterminating six million Jews," declared Khalid Abdul Muhammad the Black anti-Semite. "That's right. But don't nobody ever ask what did they do to Hitler? What did they do to them folks? They went in there, in Germany, the way they do everywhere they go, and they supplanted, they usurped, they turned around and a German, in his own country, would almost have to go to a Jew to get money. They had undermined the very fabric of the society."

Aside from rationalizing Hitler's genocidal plan, Muhammad turned against the Pope, and then all Whites. "When we gain enough power [in South Africa]," he declared, "we kill everything White that ain't right . . . we kill the women, we kill the children, we kill the babies. We kill the blind, we kill the crippled, we kill 'em all . . . and when you get through killing 'em, go to the graveyard and dig up the grave and kill 'em goddamn again. 'Cause they didn't die hard enough."

Muhammad went on to accuse Jews of killing Jesus, of running the slave trade, and of supporting apartheid. As he spewed out his anti-Semitic venom, he basked in the applause of the students and faculty who had come to hear him speak at Kean College that November 29, 1993.

Several months later I delivered a response to Muhammad at Kean. Wearing a bulletproof vest and surrounded by forty security agents, I tried to dissect his thesis point by point and demanded that the Jewish community stand up to Muhammad and his ilk. At the same time, however, I insisted that the Black community as a whole not be judged on the basis of Muhammad's violent rhetoric.

"As a rabbi, I issue this stern warning to Jews everywhere," I said. "Don't allow Mr. Muhammad's speech to turn you against Blacks. That's communal guilt. That's blaming an entire community for the bigotry and hate of one person, of one group. We dare not allow the evil of one man, of one group, to turn us against an entire race. Rather, we must peacefully confront, without bending one iota, those individuals and only those individuals, those groups and only those groups, who are racist and anti-Semitic."

This belief is a cornerstone of my activism. Implicating a whole people on the basis of wrongful acts of a few is a form of racism. Racism is discriminating against another person solely because of who he or she is. Collective guilt similarly implicates a person solely because he or she belongs to a particular group.

But does this position accord with traditional Jewish thinking? On the face of it, the Torah seems to advocate collective guilt and, for that matter, collective punishment. After all, we were mandated to kill the Amalek nation who attacked us after we left Egypt. The mandate specifically included the killing of all of Amalek—men, women, and children—even those who did not wage war upon us. Isn't that collective guilt and punishment?

Responding to this question, Rabbi Ahron Soloveichik noted that in one biblical text dealing with Amalek, the Torah in the Book of Deuteronomy says, "You (the people) will wipe out (timcheh) Amalek." In the Book of Exodus, however, God declares, "I will blot (emcheh) Amalek out." What do we learn from this seeming contradiction?

Rabbi Soloveichik concludes that the two texts complement rather than contradict one another. God is saying, you, the people, must destroy all of Amalek, but only if I, God, designate a people "Amalek"—that is, a people so evil it is worthy of annihilation.

Amalek is, therefore, an exception to the rule. In normal circumstances, communal guilt and punishment are to be deplored. In rare cases, when God or His emissary declares a people "Amalek," communal punishment is permitted.

In contemporary times, when God does not speak as He spoke in the biblical era, and God does not designate any people "Amalek," collective punishment is out of bounds. The innocent are not to be punished for the sins of the guilty.

True, Rav Yosef Dov Soloveitchik argued that the Germans of World War II can be considered figurative "Amalek," since they intended to wipe out all Jews. But Rav Soloveitchik insisted that the Biblical command to kill *all* of Amalek only applies to the Amalek nation, and that nation has been extinct for thousands of years—it did not exist even in the guise of Nazi Germany.

A contemporary example: Some years ago former Israeli Prime Minister Yitzhak Shamir said of the Poles that they imbibed anti-Semitism from their mothers' milk. If the Prime Minister meant that Poles are born with inherently anti-Semitic attitudes, he was mistaken. If, however, he meant that at a very young age, many individual Polish youths were taught anti-Semitism, which they would later act upon, then, tragically, he was correct.

Try as I have to make this point—to distinguish between specific targets of our protest and the collective whole of which the individual target is part—I have failed. In many circles I am erroneously viewed as anti-Catholic because of protests against Cardinal Glemp of Poland, anti-Muslim because of protests against Sheikh Rahman, and anti-Black because of protests against the Nation of Islam and the Reverend Louis Farrakhan. In effect, I am conveniently accused of targeting the collective, even as I struggle to pinpoint only the offending individual.

This reaction has deeply saddened me. One can raise a voice of moral conscience against particular bigots while maintaining a deep respect for the goodness of the larger group to which they belong. Our struggle against Glemp, the Sheikh, and Farrakhan are not struggles between Jews and Catholics, Jews and Muslims, or Jews and Blacks. Rather, it is a struggle between the voices of decency in all our communities and those in each community who preach hate, racism and anti-Semitism.

March 1997

Principle Five

Go After the Big Guys

When something goes awry, it's the big guy—the first man or woman—who must be called to account. Rather than tolerating a leader's tendency to transfer guilt to a subordinate, we must take a lesson from the Torah and demand of the leader—as God demanded of Adam—Ayeka (Where are you)! The readiness to speak truth to power is one of the basic principles of spiritual activism. There are far fewer consequences when dealing with lower officials who are much easier to pick off. Confronting the mighty is a far more difficult task.

To understand how people often conduct themselves when confronted with their own wrongdoing, it's worthwhile to go directly to the first recorded case of passing the buck. The Torah describes Adam's reaction when God called him to account for committing the first sin. "The woman made me do it," Adam says, kicking the blame downstairs. In turn, the woman, Eve, when confronted, also points the finger downward—to the snake.

God, however, does not let Adam get away with this. "*Ayeka?*" God says. "Where are *you*?" What have *you* done?" God does not countenance kicking the blame downstairs. Rather, He goes directly after the big guy, showing the way by challenging Adam himself.

The central principle that emerges from this is that when something goes awry, it's the big guy—the first man or woman—who must be called to account. Rather than tolerating a leader's tendency to transfer guilt to a subordinate, we must take a lesson from the Torah and demand of the leader—as God demanded of Adam—*Ayeka!* The readiness to speak truth to power is one of the basic principles of spiritual activism. There are far fewer consequences when dealing with lower officials who are much easier to pick off. Confronting the mighty is a far more difficult task.

In August of 1991, for example, when Yankele Rosenbaum was murdered during the Crown Heights riots, we went directly after the big guy. We accused New York City mayor, David Dinkins, of holding the cops back in order to allow the raging mob to vent. Our language was precise: The mayor, like all of us, saw what was happening. If he remained silent, he—not a lower level official or police captain—is culpable.

There's no question that our accusations got through to Dinkins. In one of the most successful rallies we ever mounted, a mock coffin was brought to Gracie Mansion, the mayor's official residence, as our way of placing accountability at the mayor's door. The mayor was incensed, and that evening, on the local news, accused me of racially dividing the city. But an important point was made: The man at the top was responsible. Over the ensuing period of time, a large group of activists, mostly from non-establishment grassroots organizations, led by Yankele Rosenbaum's brother, Norman, militated against the mayor until he was voted out of office.

What occurred in Argentina in July of 1994 after the AMIA Jewish community center building was bombed provides yet another illustration of this principle. During my visit to the families of the victims, someone arranged for me to see Carlos Menem, then president of Argentina. Following our one-on-one meeting, Menem invited me to a full cabinet session. There he attempted to show how his government had done all it could to find the terrorists who had destroyed the Israeli embassy in Buenos Aires two years earlier, and would do no less to find the AMIA culprits. When I communicated this information to high-level intelligence contacts, I was told that Menem's efforts were superficial and were merely designed to divert us. Thus began a campaign to expose Menem as guilty of a cover-up.

The campaign had its consequences. After laying out my allegations on a Sixty Minutes-like Argentine television program, I was summoned to the office of Chief Judge Galeano, who was investigating the AMIA explosion. He held me for six hours. This, I believe, was Menem's way through the judiciary of sending me a message—back off. We chose, however, not to get his message. Wherever Menem traveled, we tried to be there. Most notably, we showed up at an event sponsored by Rabbi Arthur Schneier's Appeal to Conscience Foundation at which Menem, of all people, was being honored. Aware of my opposition to Menem, Schneier, who had spotted me there, facilitated my arrest. Together with my colleague, Rabbi David Kalb, we were dragged down three flights of stairs head first to the waiting police van. Though we did not succeed in removing Menem from office, he knew that wherever he went the voice of moral conscience would follow him. It would follow him—not his underlings. It would follow the big guy himself.

But perhaps the most difficult case of going after the big guy related to the chairman of the United States Holocaust Memorial Museum, Miles Lerman. While Dinkins and Menem were outsiders, Lerman is part of the *mishpacha,* part of the family, and rules governing internal disputes should be softer. Still, for reasons that only he understood, Lerman was abetting the violation of Shoah memory by allowing the museum and the dead it memorialized to be politicized and universalized by such outside entities as the State Department and the Polish government. Thus, our response to Lerman had to be similar to what our response would have been to any outside, external threat.

Lerman allowed Shoah memory to be politicized when he agreed to a State Department request during Mideast negotiations to escort Yasser Arafat on a public-relations visit of the museum in order to render the Palestinian leader more acceptable to the

American-Jewish community. Turning to then director of the museum, Dr. Walter Reich—who is also my brother-in-law—and deliberately omitting the information that the invitation had already been extended, he asked whether Arafat should come. Dr. Reich advised him that Arafat should not come; it was Dr. Reich's conviction that the museum should never be used as an instrument to promote any political agenda. Lerman disinvited Arafat, but then, under pressure from the State Department, reversed. When that matter hit the press and became public, he proceeded to blame the embarrassment on Dr. Reich, who resigned in protest against the misuse of Holocaust memory.

The museum under Lerman also promoted the universalization of Shoah memory in its readiness to hire John Roth as the director of its Center for Advanced Holocaust Studies. In his writings, Roth had drawn moral equivalencies between the Nazis' treatment of Jews and Israel's treatment of Palestinians. Instead of making sure that the museum would remain a place in which the Shoah would be remembered as a unique event, Lerman opened the door for it to become a center for the indiscriminate presentation of every variety of victimization.

The most egregious example of Lerman's preparedness to promote universalization—indeed, Christianization—of Shoah memory was when, as head of a self-appointed coalition of Jewish organizations, he was ready to sign an agreement with the Polish government concerning the final status of the Auschwitz death camp in which over one million Jews were murdered. Lerman's deal would have kept in place the large cross near the old convent at Auschwitz 1, and would have let stand the church in Birkenau (Auschwitz 11), which served as SS headquarters during the war, with its large cross in front and on the roof. The Poles would never have negotiated with American Jews had Lerman, as head of a Federal institution, not brought to the table the imprimatur of the U.S. government.

Never mind that Lerman was exposing Holocaust memory to State Department pressure—the State Department that was responsible for sitting on its hands as six million Jews were murdered. Never mind that Lerman was violating the museum's narrow mandate of education and remembrance by dragging it into diplomatic negotiations with a foreign country. Somehow, like some survivors I have seen who are afflicted with a kind of Stockholm Syndrome, Lerman was falling all over the Poles, accepting awards and honors from them, looking forward to signing agreements with them at gala ceremonies. Indeed, Sen. Orin Hatch of Utah told me he had been invited to attend the signing ceremony of this agreement that was to take place in July of 1998.

And so we went after the big guy. It was painful to go against a member of the *mishpacha*, but we had no choice. We accused Lerman—the person at the top—of violating Shoah memory. In the summer of 1998, we lobbied in Congress, asking that the museum be investigated for violating its specific mandate of education and remembrance by engaging in international diplomacy; at the same time, we took great pains to stress that no Federal money be withheld from the museum in carrying out its legitimate mandate. Soon after, Congress commissioned an investigation by the National Academy of Public Administration (NAPA). The NAPA Report, when it appeared in the summer of 1999, criticized Lerman severely for his actions during the Arafat affair, and also questioned the propriety of the museum's involvement in the Auschwitz negotiations.

In the end, Arafat never came to the Museum. John Roth declined the appointment as head of its scholarly branch. Most important, the agreement with the Poles has not, to date, been signed. In addition, as a result of the publication of the NAPA Report, Lerman was forced to resign.

It is never easy to go after the person at the top. One is often alone and shunned when doing so. During our campaign against Lerman, for example, important Federation newspapers in the community, would not publish our articles on the subject for fear of antagonizing so powerful an establishment organization as the U.S. Holocaust Memorial Museum. The lesson for us is this: When the big guys won't go after a big guy who does wrong, it remains for us, the grassroots, the little guys, to take him on. When seeing a wrong, it's easy to pass the buck and kick the blame downstairs.

God's *ayeka* teaches us to call to account those who have mis-stepped no matter how high and mighty they are.

March 2000

Principle Six

Speak Out Not Only for the Living,
But Also for the Dead

Beyond the primary concern of the Jewish activist to keep the Jewish state, as well as all of the Jewish people around the world, alive and strong in body and soul, we also have an obligation to help ensure that our past is preserved intact. It follows, therefore, that activists have a responsibility to speak out for the dead, and the most vulnerable of the dead are the victims of the Holocaust, whose memory is in danger of being desecrated by Holocaust revisionists.

It was June 24, 1987, one day before Pope John Paul II was to receive Kurt Waldheim, the unrepentant Nazi who had become the president of Austria, in the pontiff's offices at the Vatican. Four of us who had come to Rome to protest the Waldheim visit marched into St. Peter's Square wearing mock concentration camp uniforms and prayer shawls and accompanied by a large entourage of reporters. As we stood beneath the Pope's balcony, one reporter asked why we were there. I responded simply, "We are here to speak for those who cannot speak for themselves."

I was referring to the six million Jewish victims of the Holocaust, some of whom had almost certainly been murdered under the watchful eye of the young Kurt Waldheim, who during World War II was a fast-rising officer in the Nazi Wehrmacht. The evidence turned up by the World Jewish Congress and others in

1986 was overwhelming that Waldheim, who would eventually go on to serve for a decade as secretary general of the United Nations, had helped facilitate the deportation of the Jews of Salonika to Auschwitz when he served in that Greek city, and that he took part in Nazi massacres of civilians in Yugoslavia. I was also seeking to remind the Church and the entire world that by honoring Waldheim, Pope John Paul II was playing directly into the hands of the Holocaust revisionists who were seeking to murder the Six Million a second time by denying that the Shoah ever happened.

There is no question that the primary function of the activist is to speak out for and give succor to the living. Therefore the ultimate response of the Jewish activist to the unfathomable horror of the Shoah, the fiendish campaign to erase our people from the earth forever, must be to do whatever he or she can to strengthen the living State of Israel. While there is considerable debate as to whether the modern Jewish state would have been born if the Holocaust had not happened, there can be little doubt that had Israel existed by the 1930s, there would never have been a Holocaust. Therefore, in the grim aftermath of the annihilation of a third of our people, we have a unique responsibility to see to it that the State of Israel, which is essential to the continuation of our very existence as a people, remains strong and vibrant.

We must also do our share to help Israel recognize its special mission as a light unto the nations of the world. The real challenge facing the Jewish state, once its safety is assured, involves deciding what kind of state it will ultimately become. Will it exist as a democracy where many Jews happen to live, or as a uniquely Jewish state that is also a democracy?

Yet beyond the primary concern of the Jewish activist to keep the Jewish state, as well as all of the Jewish people around the world, alive and strong in body and soul, we also have an obligation to help ensure that our past is preserved intact. Rav Yosef Dov Soloveitchik makes this point in general terms when he defines *hesed* as any act of kindness which helps the other, adding that the more the recipient is unable to help himself or herself, the greater the act of kindness. From that perspective, he asked his students what the greatest act of kindness is? Some responded that it is helping the sick, especially the most innocent, such as infants. That is indeed a great act of kindness, Rav Soloveitchik replied, but even more defenseless than infants are the dead, who can in no way help themselves. Caring for them is therefore called a *hesed shel emet*, an act of true kindness.

It follows, therefore, that activists have a responsibility to speak out for the dead, and the most vulnerable of the dead are the victims of the Holocaust, whose memory is in danger of being desecrated by Holocaust revisionists. It is for this reason that activists have a responsibility to fight vigorously to preserve, as intact as possible, the former Nazi death camps, where so many of our people breathed their last. Over the past decade and a half, convents, parish churches, and chapels have been established at the sites of several of the former death camps, while the remains of most of the camps continue to decay.

It is possible that fifty years from now all that will be left at Auschwitz-Birkenau and other camps will be Christian, largely Catholic, symbols and houses of worship. People may then come to assume that the Holocaust was an attempt at the genocide of Catholics, or that the Vatican courageously fought to protect Jews from their Nazi tormentors. The truth is that not only did the Vatican largely fail to help Jews, but it actually assisted Nazis to flee to places of refuge after the war. While we hold out our hands in friendship and respect to Christians and to all good people of faith, we declare loudly and clearly that Christian Holocaust revisionism is just as unacceptable as any other kind.

In addition to guarding the sanctity of the death camps, activists must also insist that Holocaust museums around the world, including the U.S. Holocaust Memorial Museum in Washington, should be dedicated to recording the unique Jewish tragedy of the Shoah and not become museums for "All Suffering." They should never be allowed to become venues where the Shoah is politicized or universalized in support of any-one's particular human rights agenda.

Most important, activists must insist that the Shoah become part of Jewish ritual. There is nothing in Jewish history that is remembered today that has not been ritualized. We remember Egyptian slavery because of the Passover seder, and Haman's attempt to annihilate the Jewish people in Persia because of the Purim holiday. Without a similar type of religious observance developed uniquely for the Shoah, a hundred years from now I fear the Holocaust will become little more than a footnote in Jewish history. We at *Amcha* and at our synagogue, the Hebrew Institute of Riverdale, have made modest strides in the ritualiza-tion of the Shoah. *Amcha* has produced a "Haggadah for the Yom HaShoah Seder" which is used on Holocaust Memorial Day. And, every Shabbat at our synagogue we follow a practice first intro-duced by Rabbi Saul Berman. Before the reading of *"Av HaRachamim,"* the prayer commemorating the victims of the Crusades, a congregant reads a sixty second vignettte about a European shtetl that was and no longer is—having been destroyed by the Nazis.

And, of course, we must continue to be relentless in our pur-suit of former Nazis. Those who participated in the darkest evil of human history cannot be forgiven or forgotten. They cannot be for-given because only the six million Jews who perished in the Shoah have the right to forgive, and they are no longer with us. They can-not be forgotten, because as George Santayana noted, "Those who do not remember the past are condemned to relive it."

No matter how wealthy or powerful, no matter how well pro-tected or highly placed these former Nazis may be, activists have a responsibility to confront these people, expose the truth about their pasts, and demand that they finally be made to pay for their crimes. We must do this whether the war criminal is Valerian Trifa, a former head of the Romanian Iron Guard, who hanged two hundred Jews from meat hooks in Bucharest Square in January 1941 only to become the archbishop of Detroit, Michigan; or John

Demjanjuk, who murdered thousands in Treblinka and Sobibor yet gained the sympathy of thousands as he returned from Israel to a hero's welcome in Ohio. We must even do so when that criminal is someone as renowned as Kurt Waldheim, who facilitated the murder of thousands in Yugoslavia and Greece and then went on to become secretary general of the United Nations and president of Austria.

We activists have a sacred responsibility to protect the dead by following their murderers wherever they go. We will not rest while one Nazi criminal who has escaped justice is still out there—no matter how old or infirm. And when these monsters are finally gone, we must redouble our efforts to ensure that their genocidal crimes are never forgotten.

May 1998

MAKING PARTNERS

The Spiritual Activist seeks to work with the larger Jewish community—with rabbis, with Jews of all denominations, with the young and the old, and with non-Jews.

The Spiritual Activist avoids certain potential allies by refusing to accept financial support from those who have gained their wealth unethically, or by blindly following established leaders.

The Spiritual Activist recognizes that, in the realm of pure spirit, everyone has something to offer.

Principle Seven

The Jewish Community Is a Symphony

We view the Jewish community as a symphony orchestra in which there are drummers, flutists, violinists, and so on. We are drummers, peaceful drummers; our goal is not to drown out the flutists and violinists, but to beat steadily, relentlessly, never stopping, and yes, sometimes sounding the alarm loud and clear. When any one of the instruments is missing, there is no symphony. Each one has an important place in the orchestra.

When the Reverend Martin Luther King, Jr. demonstrated peacefully for civil rights in the South, local Black leadership was asked to stop him. At first they marginalized him. Later they learned the valuable lesson of community orchestration. When asked to dissociate themselves from Reverend King, they responded: "His style is not our style. However, he's a peaceful man, he has a following, and his cause is correct. We can't stop him. You can stop him. All you have to do is give our people more rights."

In sharp contrast to this lesson are the circumstances surrounding the recent protests outside the NAACP summit in Baltimore. There, *Tikkun* editor Michael Lerner, Michael Meyers, a former assistant national director of the NAACP, and I joined forces to protest the NAACP's embrace of Reverend Louis Farrakhan. Our quarrel was not with the African-American community, but rather with a particular bigot and with those who had sought to legitimize him.

Unfortunately, in the days before the summit, the Baltimore Jewish Council announced its opposition to any protests. In the words of its director, "This may inflame and provoke rather than attempt to heal the discord between the African-American and Jewish communities." Through the first two days of the summit we continued our protests, including a synagogue rally that drew more than 500 enthusiastic supporters.

This reaction by the Baltimore Jewish Council was reminiscent of a similar event a few years back. In 1989, after we demonstrated outside the Auschwitz convent, Cardinal Josef Glemp of Poland publicly proclaimed that we had come to kill the nuns. With the help of Alan Dershowitz, we sued him for defamation. We reached a point where Cardinal Glemp was about to sign a carefully worded statement of apology for anti-Semitic remarks, a statement that would have represented a momentous breakthrough in Jewish-Christian relations. The day before he was to sign the statement, two leaders of the American Jewish Congress arrived in Poland and told Cardinal Glemp that I had "contribut[ed] to anti-Semitism in Poland" and had acted "destructively and in an irresponsible manner." Cardinal Glemp then refused to sign the apology on the grounds that his accusation had been validated by these two Jewish leaders.

The appropriate reaction of these leaders should have been to follow the example set in the civil rights movement. The Jewish establishment should have said: "His way is not our way. However, he is a peaceful man, he has a following, and his cause is just. We can't stop him. You can. You can stop him by removing the convent."

Long ago the great medieval poet and philosopher Rabbi Judah HaLevi, in his *Kuzari*, compared the Jewish people in certain ways to a symphony orchestra. We too view the Jewish community as a symphony orchestra in which there are drummers, flutists, violinists, and so on. We are drummers, peaceful drummers; our goal is not to drown out the flutists and violinists, but to beat steadily, relentlessly, never stopping, and yes, sometimes sounding the alarm loud and clear. When any one of the instruments is missing, there is no symphony. Each one has an important place in the orchestra. Natan Sharansky, just a few days after arriving on his first U.S. visit, said it best: "Quiet diplomacy can help only if it is supported by strong public pressure."

Case in point: When Pat Buchanan was running for president, a number of rabbis—Orthodox, Conservative, and Reform— joined in raising a voice against his anti-Semitic and racist statements. At his final "America First" rally on the eve of the Georgia primary, I called out, "You anti-Semitism makes America last." He looked down at us and replied, "This is a rally of Americans, for Americans and for the good old USA, my friends." Translation: Jews, if you don't like it, get out of here.

The very next day both the American Jewish Congress and the American Jewish Committee, to their credit, released statements asserting that it was now clear that Pat Buchanan is an anti-Semite. Here the activists and the establishment worked together, and the discord of Buchanan's offensive statements was stilled by the harmony of the Jewish community.

For years I have said that our brand of activism is not anti-establishment but rather non-establishment. I understand the position of those like the Baltimore Jewish Council in the case of the NAACP-Farrakhan protest. However, its approach is no more or less legitimate than ours, which is to take direct action in a peaceful manner. The Baltimore Jewish Council has a right to its opinion as a member of the Jewish community, but it steps beyond the line when it declares that its way is the only way.

Rabbi Judah HaLevi, in comparing the Jewish people to a symphony orchestra, wrote that congregational prayer, the prayer of the group, is more powerful than private prayer. In group prayer, one individual's deficiency is compensated for by another's strength. In private prayer, the deficiency remains glaring. Similarly, we must all stand beside and complement those groups in our community whose methods of speaking out differ from our own. There must be mutual recognition that as much as *amcha*—the grassroots—needs the establishment, the establishment needs *amcha*.

July 1994

Principle Eight

Rabbis Should Play a Leading Role in Activism

Asked what the function of a rabbi is, Rabbi Hayyim of Brisk replied: "To redress the grievances of those who are abandoned and alone, to protect the dignity of the poor, and to save the oppressed from the hands of his oppressor." For Rabbi Hayyim of Brisk, standing up for righteousness and speaking out for justice are the pillars of the rabbinate. It's an idea all rabbis should embrace.

When Rabbi Abraham Joshua Heschel and Reverend Martin Luther King, Jr. marched together in Selma, Alabama, their action expressed the responsibility that spiritual leaders bear to transform the world. Yet in our day, too few rabbis are involved in social or political action, and those who do engage in such activities are often derided and marginalized. For example, one would imagine that rabbis, in the spirit of Heschel, would be welcomed onto the national boards of directors of major Jewish defense agencies. But a cursory review of the leadership of the Anti-Defamation League, the American Jewish Committee, and the American Jewish Congress reveals just the opposite. Very few congregational rabbis are included, and that has been the case with few exceptions over the past fifty years of American Jewish life.

Why is this so?

In pre-war Europe, especially in Germany, "secular" Jews relegated rabbis to the study hall and the synagogue. Rabbis dealt with the world of the spirit; Jewish organizations dealt with the world of politics. The two worlds were separate and distinct.

This attitude has been carried over to America. The key defense agencies, which not coincidentally are the strictest interpreters of the separation of church and state doctrine, believe that rabbis should remain ensconced within the spiritual confines of the synagogue. They will do everything to protect the rabbi's right to be there, to teach Torah, to spread the word of God—as long as the rabbi remains more or less within the realm of the spiritual.

It shouldn't be this way. Rabbi Avraham Yitzhak HaKohen Kook, the first chief rabbi of Israel, argued that there is no such thing as the unholy; there is only the holy and the not yet holy. From this perspective, everyday life—the way one eats, works, and, yes, engages in politics—is as holy as prayer, Torah study, and meditation. For Rav Kook, speaking out for *Am Yisrael* is, in its purest form, the deepest expression of Jewish spirituality. And no one is in a better position to sanctify the political process than are the rabbis. As people of the spirit, they are trained to infuse all aspects of life with spirituality.

If we also bear in mind that activism is a gateway to the stirring of Jewish consciousness, it becomes even more obvious why rabbis are well suited to lead such efforts. Who better than rabbis, learned in Torah, know and recognize how Jewish activism can inspire unaffiliated Jews to become more identified with their people?

There is another reason why rabbis should play a central role in the political leadership of *Am Yisrael*. Rabbis are leaders of synagogues—the institutions that are most in touch with the grassroots—and thus have the capacity both to lead their followers and to reflect their views. When the UJA wishes to galvanize the Jewish community, it is not to the defense agencies that it turns, but to synagogues and their rabbis. UJA recognizes that it is the rabbis who have the most direct contact with and influence upon the people. Rabbis, more than anyone else, can effectively issue a call to action. More than anyone else, they represent the *amcha*, or people.

Despite this fact, the views of rabbis are too often disregarded. For example, as part of the campaign for Jonathan Pollard's freedom, the Coalition for Jewish Concerns/*Amcha* galvanized one thousand rabbis—including the presidents of the Orthodox, Conservative, Reform and Reconstructionist rabbinical schools and rabbinical organizations—who signed an open letter to the U.S. president declaring that Pollard's sentence was excessive and should be commuted to time served. Asked about the impact of this letter, a key leader of the American Jewish Congress said, "This doesn't represent the Jewish people."

I vividly remember Jonathan Pollard's reaction to this comment. Lowering his eyes, he asked: "The real question this raises concerns Jewish empowerment. Who speaks for the Jewish people?" It is my contention, as it was Pollard's that day, that it is the rabbis who best give voice to the people's will.

It is not the fault of the Jewish defense agencies alone that rabbis are shunted aside. Rabbis must also bear the blame. Too many of my colleagues share the belief that the world of the spirit should be separated from the world of politics. Too many of my colleagues believe that the only way to teach is through words, theories, and ideas, when in fact the best sermon is the way one acts and not the way one preaches. Too many of my colleagues shy away from taking strong political positions, fearful that they will alienate their boards and congregants. They forget the warning of the holy Ba'al Shem Tov, that a rabbi who is loved by everyone is a failing rabbi.

A wise, elderly man taught me this lesson. On the day I left my first pulpit in St. Louis, he approached me and said, "Rabbi, I bless you that you should have many enemies." I looked at him, startled. "We've been close, why such a cruel blessing?" "My words are meant as a blessing," he responded. "Remember, if you do nothing, you have no enemies. A sign that you're doing, that you're taking stands, is that you have enemies."

I've often been criticized for wearing a *tallit* (prayer shawl) at demonstrations around the world. A leader from one of the major

Jewish organizations wrote to me, "A *tallit* is meant for synagogues, not for activism." I respectfully disagree. For the world at
large, the *tallit* identifies its wearer as a rabbi. I want all to know
that rabbis take the lead in defending Jews. Interestingly, at the
recent commemoration at Auschwitz, marking the fiftieth anniversary of its liberation, the World Jewish Congress asked all participants to wear prayer shawls as they entered the camp.

Asked what the function of a rabbi is, Rabbi Hayyim of Brisk
replied, "To redress the grievances of those who are abandoned
and alone, to protect the dignity of the poor, and to save the
oppressed from the hands of his oppressor." For Rabbi Hayyim of
Brisk, standing up for righteousness and speaking out for justice
are the pillars of the rabbinate. It's an idea that Heschel and King
learned well. It's one that all rabbis should embrace, and Jewish
defense agencies should in turn welcome these rabbis into their
leadership and onto their boards.

March 1995

Principle Nine

Orthodox, Conservative and Reform Jews
Should Work Together

Speaking at the fortieth anniversary of the Synagogue Council of America in 1967, Dr. Samuel Belkin, the late president of Yeshiva University, said: "In the things which we fully agree upon and in which all of us are deeply concerned, we are the most united people in the world. If Russian Jewry is denied the religious liberty to bake matzos for Pesach . . . if the borders of the State of Israel are threatened . . . if an anti-Semitic movement generates in any part of the world, all Jews are united as one." In the past few years I've come to see that there are more opportunities for the movements to interact. Consciously or not, we have all learned from each other.

A few weeks ago, during a rally in which I participated with forty Orthodox rabbis opposing U.S. funding for the PLO, our spokesman declared, "We represent the American rabbinate." When a journalist asked how the group represented the American rabbinate when there were no Conservative or Reform rabbis present, the spokesman indicated that non-Orthodox rabbis are not authentic rabbis.

I was taken aback. Despite my personal belief that Orthodoxy is the only halakhically legitimate expression of Judaism and my recognition that the other expressions are shaped by their rabbis, I was distressed by my colleague's comments.

Synagogues and temples representing millions of Conservative, Reform, and Reconstructionist Jews are found everywhere in the United States. To negate their spiritual mentors is to insult all of non-Orthodox Jewry. It suggests that in the eyes of Orthodoxy, those movements do not exist, when of course they do.

For the ultimate good of American Jewry, it would be wise for the rabbis of all the movements to adopt a moratorium on the spirit of negativism directed at other movements. Emphasis should be placed on who we are rather than on who the other is not. We should focus on our positive values rather than on the other's "negatives."

Beyond the question of the relationship with other rabbis, Orthodoxy has also confronted the larger question of its relationship with other movements. Two positions have emerged. One is to avoid contact so as not to give the non-Orthodox legitimacy. It was for this reason that the rabbis who assembled at the Washington rally were all Orthodox. The group had received a *psak*, a halakhic decision, that while they could work with Evangelical Christians, non-Orthodox rabbis were *verboten*.

Dr. Samuel Belkin, the late president of Yeshiva University, looked at it differently. Speaking at the fortieth anniversary of the Synagogue Council of America in 1967, Dr. Belkin said: "Some say that the main goal of the Synagogue Council is to help in creating a spirit of unity in the American Jewish community. Here . . . I disagree. In the things in which we differ we can have no unity, nor should it be expected of us, . . . particularly of Jews of Orthodox orientation. In the things which we fully agree upon and in which all of us are deeply concerned, we are the most united people in the world. If Russian Jewry is denied the religious liberty to bake matzos for Pesach . . . if the borders of the State of Israel are threatened . . . if an anti-Semitic movement generates in any part of the world, all Jews are united as one."

I thought about Dr. Belkin's words on my first visit to Buenos Aires a year ago, following the bombing of the AMIA Jewish Cultural Center. I had gone there to give comfort to the injured and to the families of the bereaved. During that difficult period, the Orthodox community called for a prayer service and made a point of listing only Orthodox rabbis.

Many Conservative Jews approached me and said: "That bomb was meant for all Jews, not just for the Orthodox. Shouldn't we, the entire Jewish community, have found a way of gathering together?"

Certainly the same argument could have been made concerning the demonstrations of the rabbis in Washington. We were there to protest the funding of an organization that does not differentiate between Orthodox and non-Orthodox in its terror. The goal is to murder Jews; the denominational label is irrelevant.

I have always sought to conduct myself in accordance with Dr. Belkin's principle. I have stood together with non-Orthodox colleagues, raising a voice of Jewish concern. But in these past few years, I've come to see that there are more opportunities for the movements to interact. Consciously or not, we have all learned from each other.

- The Orthodox movement has in some measure emulated the Conservative movement 's model of the synagogue as a Jewish community center.
- The Reform and the Conservative movements' greater sensitivity to day school education and increased emphasis on ritual and learning Torah in Jewish life have much to do with Orthodox influence.

There is still much more to be learned.

- Orthodox Jewry should adopt elements of the Reform and Reconstructionist universalist agenda of *tikkun olam*, or a commitment to "repair of the world."
- Reform would be strengthened if it experimented with the notion of *mitzvah* as the state of being "commanded," as understood by Orthodox Jewry.

A final consideration needs to be incorporated into our vision. For the Jewish community to truly flourish, it is not only the Orthodox who must show respect for the non-Orthodox, but the reverse must also hold.

How vividly I recall a Lubavitch rally after the acquittal of Lemrick Nelson, Jr., for the Yankele Rosenbaum murder. At a demonstration sponsored by Lubavitch, men and women assembled in separate areas. A prominent non-Orthodox rabbi complained that he was treated improperly. After all, the women who had accompanied him to the rally were asked to stand in the women's section. Why, the rabbi wondered, wasn't it mixed? On his radio talk show, former Mayor Ed Koch, a non-Orthodox Jew, reacted indignantly, pointing out that it was a Lubavitch event. Therefore, their customs, he correctly argued, had to be respected.

In the words of Rav Avraham Yitzhak HaKohen Kook, "What unites us is far greater than what divides us." These simple but powerful words should be taken seriously by the broad spectrum of the Jewish community.

August 1995

Principle Ten

Youthful Brashness and Naiveté
Can Have Great Impact

Isaiah carefully describes the Messianic period. It will be a time when "a wolf will dwell with a lamb, and a leopard will lie with a kid." And then he adds the immortal words—"*ve-na'ar katon noheg otam*; a young lad will lead them." Isaiah understood that redemption requires those who are energized, those who are bold, those who dream—in short, our young people. That's the way it has been in recent years. The civil rights movement, the anti-war (Vietnam) movement, were all started by young people. And, so too, was the case in the Soviet and Ethiopian Jewry movements. It was the young—brash, naïve but strong who, in Isaiah's words, led the way.

When I meet students I taught thirty years ago, I occasionally have the urge to apologize.

After all, I ask myself, what knowledge could I have possessed when I was such a young man that could have had a positive impact on these students? I knew so little in those days. Looking back, I wish I could have taught with a bit more of the wisdom that comes with age.

Yet on a number of occasions when I have had the opportunity to express these sentiments to students of mine from two to three decades ago, they have answered that they had found my

classes meaningful. Their earnest responses have led me to conclude that in different phases of life, people bring different
strengths to the table. When we are young, we may be less knowledgeable, but the enthusiasm and zeal of youth can compensate
for the relative lack of wisdom. The willingness that a young person has to take a passionate, unambiguous stand on behalf of a certain truth sometimes affords a once-in-a-lifetime opportunity to
make an impact on the world; that very same person, when older,
may often be less convinced of the absolute righteousness of the
cause in question.

Looking back on those long-ago days when I would stand in
front of my students shoeless and with an open shirt, speaking at
high-decibel levels and gesticulating dramatically, utterly
enthralled by the material I felt privileged to transmit, I realize that
my lectures may have been loud and less informed by mature
reflection, but they were nevertheless exciting. As we studied the
simple commentaries—because that was all I knew well enough to
teach at the time—I was able to communicate to my students the
meaning at the heart of these interpretations, and to do so with a
joyful exuberance that was not only energizing to my listeners, but
sometimes inspiring as well.

As the years have flown by, the passion of youth that I once
possessed, has, alas, diminished, while my ability to express complex ideas to my students with greater precision and insight has
grown with maturity. Just as my youthful exuberance fired up my
students of a generation ago, I hope that the strengths I have
acquired as an older and, yes, wiser teacher in middle age have
made a positive difference for the students I have had the privilege
to work with in more recent years.

A similar dynamic applies in the world of spiritual activism. A
young activist leader often speaks out with a brashness bordering
on arrogance, a know-it-all attitude, a belief in the certainty that
there is nothing that cannot be accomplished. Years later, imbued
with an increased understanding of the world that comes with
maturity, that same leader often comes to the painful realization

that there are limits to what can be achieved by any single individual. Filled with an awareness that one does not, after all, possess a monopoly on wisdom and truth—indeed, one of my fundamental principles of activism is to be wary of anyone who is certain, absolutely certain that his or her way is without doubt the only correct one—the leader becomes more willing to consider the views of others. When an activist leader is young, there is nothing that seems beyond bounds to ask, or even demand, of followers. An older leader, on the other hand, often searches long and hard for the justification to ask others to sacrifice for the cause.

Both youthful brashness and mature thoughtfulness are manifestations of complementary strengths, which is why a successful activist organization or movement needs a mix of young and old. There is great value for a movement in youthful anger and naiveté. They cause people to be unafraid to speak out. The "know-it-all" attitude of young activists, harnessed to the greater insight and reflectiveness of their older counterparts, represents a formidable combination that can give a movement the means to realize the results it seeks to achieve.

Here are some examples of my "youthful" impetuousness, which shielded me, to some degree, from a full realization of the implications of what I and my fellow protesters were doing. In 1980, for example, my zealousness led me to a dramatic action when I led a group that heckled President Jimmy Carter at an appearance he made at a Queens synagogue during that year's presidential primary season. While the President, the rabbi and assorted dignitaries cringed on the stage, I jumped up in the audience and shouted that Carter had made an obscene comparison by likening the Palestine Liberation Organization to the American Civil Rights movement of the 1960s. When the President responded by expressing support for Israel, I brazenly shouted, "Carter is a liar." Today, I doubt I would have the chutzpah to shout down the President of the United States. Yet looking back from a distance of twenty years, I believe that a stand needed to be taken and only a young activist could have taken it. I also believe my action had the effect of helping to some degree to solidify Jewish opposition to Carter. At that time the Jewish community was frightened to challenge a sitting President who was perceived to be vindictive to boot. Once we spoke out against Carter publicly and said what so many were thinking, it emboldened others to publicly oppose him. Carter subsequently lost the New York primary to Ted Kennedy and the election to Ronald Reagan.

The brashness of my interruption was noticed by my mother who called from Israel that evening. "I saw you on TV," she said. "Did you have to yell Carter is a liar?" "Well he is," I responded. "You may be right," my mother responded, "but couldn't you have respectfully called out, Mr. President, you're not telling the truth!" Therein lies the difference between the impetuousness of youthful bravado and the mature voice of reasoned wisdom. But who is to say that each does not have its place in the symphony of spiritual activism.

Another instance when I followed my "youthful" instincts came in Geneva in 1985 during the first Reagan Gorbachev Summit when I asked a question at a press conference of Seagrams CEO and World Jewish Congress (WJC) President Edgar Bronfman. In my question, I charged him with working to end U.S. adherence to the Jackson-Vanik Amendment, which stipulated that the U.S. should trade freely only with those countries that accord basic human rights to their citizens. As journalists scribbled away and Bronfman sat there looking mortified, I suggested that he wanted to accord "Most Favored Nation" trading status to the Soviet Union, even though it denied Jews the right to emigrate to Israel and repressed all manifestations of Jewish culture, because Seagrams was monetarily invested in that country.

In retrospect, I may not have been fair to Bronfman. While my information indicated that Bronfman was doing business with the Soviets, he denied this claiming that he did not make enough from the Russians to pay for gas from his hotel room to the airport. And even if Bronfman was invested, I did not know for sure that he was allowing Seagram's interests in the Soviet Union to cause him to take a soft policy toward the Soviet government in his role as president of the WJC. Still, there was a reasonable inference to draw. Certainly I believed that Bronfman was eager to do more business with the Soviets. Hence, I felt an obligation to ask the question. Raising it publicly forced the WJC and other establishment Jewish groups to exercise extreme caution before advocating the deep-sixing of Jackson-Vanik

Bronfman never forgot that moment. Fourteen years later, it was arranged that I meet him at a private luncheon. His first words upon seeing me were, "You so and so, you accused me of ditching Jackson-Vanick for my benefit." It was clear that my little demonstration—carried out with youthful abandon—had lasting impact.

Isaiah carefully describes the Messianic period. It will be a time, he said, when "a wolf will dwell with a lamb, and a leopard will lie with a kid." And then he adds the immortal words, "*ve-na'ar katon noheg otam*, a young lad will lead them."Isaiah understood that redemption requires those who are energized, those who are bold, those who dream—in short, our young people. That's the way it has been in recent years. The civil rights movement, the anti-war (Vietnam) movement, were all started by young people. And so too was the case in the Soviet and Ethiopian Jewry movements. It was the young—brash, naïve but strong who in Isaiah's words, led the way.

October 1999

Principle Eleven

Older Adults Play a Crucial Role
in Spiritual Activism

It should not be forgotten that during the Exodus from Egypt, perhaps the ultimate act of activism in the history of our people, Moses insisted that the young and old leave together. In fact, Moses was eighty years old when he led the Jews out of Egypt. Over the centuries too, many of the most distinguished statesmen and most indomitable activists have made their finest contributions in their later years. While older folks may not be as physically strong as the young, they can contribute in ways that the young cannot. In the end, activism is an intergenerational symphony in which people of all ages play an indispensable role in the making of the melody.

Seated in her wheelchair, decked out in her finest, Sophie seemed content. She had just turned ninety and was being feted by her children at a gala celebration. Called upon to offer words of blessing, I concluded with the traditional *Bis hunderd un zvanzig*, "Until one hundred and twenty years." Without skipping a beat, Sophie snapped back, *Shelt mir nisht*, "Don't curse me."

What did she mean? Was she saying that one hundred and twenty years is not long enough? Or was she suggesting that to live so long would be a curse?

To be sure, length of days is considered a blessing in the Torah and is mentioned as a reward for good deeds. The Talmud insists that the utmost respect must be shown to the elderly. For example, the law is in accordance with Issi ben Yehudah, who argues that the biblical mandate to rise before the elderly refers to all old people, even those unlearned. After all, wisdom is a function not only of what one knows but also of life experiences, which the elderly certainly possess.

In fact, the Talmud speaks of two categories of caring: *kibbud* (respect) and *morah* (fear). *Kibbud* is associated with physically providing for the elderly—feeding them, dressing them, and, if necessary, carrying them in and out. *Morah*, on the other hand, is metaphysical. Do not stand or sit in their place or contradict their words.

These obligations are characteristic of a Jewish approach to the elderly which differs dramatically from the one that is the norm in American society today. Rabbi Benjamin Bleich argues that by and large, in America the elderly are cut off from the rest of society. As Americans become older, society expects less of them. As a consequence, the elderly soon come to expect less of themselves and, in time, what the elderly are conditioned to believe becomes the reality—they do less. Sadly, our culture copes with the elderly by giving them less importance. This loss of status yields a policy of isolation in which the elderly are kept out of sight, in their homes, institutions, or retirement centers.

Edith Stern, in her book *Burned Alive*, makes this very point. She writes: "Unlike some primitive tribes, we do not kill off our aged and infirm. We bury them alive in institutions. To save our face, we call the institutions 'homes'—a travesty of the word. I have seen dozens of such homes in the last six months—desolate places, peopled with blank men and women, one home so like the other that each visit seemed a recurrent nightmare."

One need only watch an evening of television commercials to recognize that what Stern wrote almost fifty years ago is still standard operating procedure in America. Commercials accentuate beauty, strength, and above all youth. Products are rarely promoted by elderly people.

Judaism sees it differently. The elderly are viewed as creative. Even those whose physical or mental capacities are limited contribute to society, for they have the potential to bring out the best in those who care for them. Hence Judaism encourages interaction with the elderly and grants them status, in the spirit of "Ask your parents and they will tell you, ask the elderly and they will teach you."

Rabbi Abraham Joshua Heschel expresses the idea this way: "May I suggest that man's potential for change and growth is much greater than we are willing to admit and that old age be regarded not as the age of stagnation, but as the age of opportunities for inner growth. The years of old age may enable us to attain the high values we have failed to sense, the insights we have missed, the wisdom we have ignored. They are indeed formative years, rich in possibilities to unlearn the follies of a lifetime, to see through inbred self-deceptions, to deepen understanding and compassion, to widen the horizon of honesty, to refine the sense of fairness."

All too often, however, Jewish institutions, including synagogues, behave in ways that make clear they have been influenced by the American approach to dealing with the elderly. Consider the proliferation throughout the country over recent years of prayer services for young couples only. Unintentionally, these services perpetuate the policy of segregating the young from the old. This tendency toward "specialized services" has far-reaching consequences. Often the children of these young people come to synagogue only when these specialized services are held. How sad it is to consider that, during their most impressionable years, so many of our children may never see the smiles or tears of an older person in shul. The reverse is also true; seniors are robbed of the opportunity to interact with children or young adults. Eleanor Roosevelt was correct when she said that the secret to staying young is to surround oneself with young people.

Similarly, we too often separate the old from the young in the realm of activism. Many assume that activism is solely a youthful enterprise. To be sure, it has been younger people who have inspired and led many of the major activist movements of contemporary times. The prime movers of the civil rights and anti-war movements of the 1960s were young people, as were many of the leaders of the struggles on behalf of Soviet Jewry and Ethiopian Jewry. Isaiah the prophet predicted that in the time of Messiah, redemption would arise through "the lads who lead the way." The prophets recognized that the innocence, energy, idealism, and sometimes naiveté of the young make them a crucial component in *tikkun olam* (fixing the world).

Nevertheless, it should not be forgotten that during the Exodus from Egypt, perhaps the ultimate act of activism in the history of our people, Moses insisted that the young and old leave together. In fact, Moses was eighty years old when he led the Jews out of Egypt. Over the centuries too, many of the most distinguished statesmen and most indomitable activists have made their finest contributions in their later years. While older folks may not be as physically strong as the young, they can contribute in ways that the young cannot. In the end, activism is an intergenerational symphony in which people of all ages play an indispensable role in the making of the melody.

How vividly I remember Bob Birnbaum—Reb Baruch, as I affectionately called him—a "simple" and unpretentious Jew in his late seventies who marched with me and a small group of activists in front of the Seven Hills, Ohio home of John Demjanjuk, in September 1993. Our demonstration took place only days after Demjanjuk returned from imprisonment in Israel to a hero's welcome in the Cleveland suburb where he had lived for many years. The Israeli Supreme Court had ruled weeks earlier that Demjanjuk was to be freed because the prosecution had failed to prove beyond a shadow of a doubt that he was really the man once known as Ivan the Terrible, the fiendish prison camp guard who tortured and killed thousands of Jews in the Treblinka death camp. Still the Supreme Court did determine that Demjanjuk was involved in the murder of thousands of Jews at the Sobibor camp, and that he also served in Trawniki, the notorious camp where Nazi guards were trained to maim and murder.

Allowed to leave Israel on legal technicalities, Demjanjuk, a Ukrainian-American, was nevertheless widely viewed by his Seven Hills neighbors, who were predominantly ethnic Ukrainian themselves, as a victim of Israeli and Jewish injustice. The leaders of the Cleveland Jewish community agreed with us that Demjanjuk was guilty of murder, but they opposed demonstrations at Demjanjuk's home out of fear that these acts would spark increased anti-Semitism in the area. Only a few Cleveland-area Jews had the courage and conviction to join us in the protest in Seven Hills. One of them was Reb Baruch, who informed me when I met him that, as a survivor of the death camps himself, he felt a moral obligation to take a stand against Demjanjuk.

As we marched back and forth in front of Demjanjuk's home, jeered at by some of his neighbors and trailed by a large contingent of media people, Reb Baruch paused suddenly in front of the television cameras and rolled up his sleeve. Turning toward Demjanjuk's home, he held up his arm and cried out: "Demjanjuk, you say you're the victim. Look at my number. I am the victim."

It was a searingly powerful moment, which none of us who stood together with Reb Baruch will ever forget. With his few well-timed words, he hammered home to Demjanjuk and the Seven Hills community the point that we as Jews will never forget or forgive those who savagely murdered our brothers and sisters, that the passage of time does not render clean the unrepentant Demjanjuk and his ilk. Reb Baruch also had a message for the Cleveland Jewish community, of which he was a part. He was telling his friends and neighbors: "Don't be afraid. If we have learned anything from the Shoah, it is that the *sha-shtil* mentality does not work. Stand up for your convictions."

After Reb Baruch made his statement, a reporter asked, "I hear you clearly, sir, but what will happen when you are gone? Who then will speak out?" Instantly and almost surreally, a teenage girl, Devorah Pomerantz, who had joined our numbers together with her classmates from Bet Sefer Mizrachi stepped forward and declared: "We will. We will bear witness."

There, in one electric moment, was a tableau of two Jews, old and young, standing together with courage and integrity to speak the truth on behalf of our people. Reb Baruch has since left this world, but for those who heard his voice that day, his message and that of the young woman who stood beside him will always be an inspiration and an example to emulate. I would hope, too, that those among us who tend to think of the elderly as being over the hill and of little use to the community will ponder what Reb Baruch did that day in Seven Hills. They ought to remember also that, it is hoped, they too will become older.

These same people might do well to consider that the section of the Torah in which we are mandated to honor the elderly concludes with a declaration by God that "I am the Lord." Why are these seemingly unrelated concepts placed in juxtaposition? Commentators suggest that God is telling us here that since He is the oldest in the universe, He is particularly concerned about those who share this divine quality and about the way they are treated.

The test of the community is the way it treats its most vulnerable—a category that often includes the elderly. If the vulnerable are mistreated, then not only are they, the victims being harmed. The victimizers lose too, and so does the community. Also God Himself is hurt, because when we disrespect the elderly, we show disrespect for God Himself.

Our challenge then becomes to make sure that when the Sophies of this world say, *shelt mir nisht*, they mean that life is so beautiful, and they are so valued and respected, that one hundred and twenty years are not enough.

November 1997

Principle Twelve

Non-Jews Can Play a Crucial Role

In my earliest years as an activist, I was unable to imagine reaching out for support from people who were not Jewish. The teachings I had imbibed as a youth had left their mark on me. I believed that non-Jews simply could not be trusted. Fortunately, it didn't take me long to recognize how wrongheaded that outlook was. Early on in my career as an activist, and on numerous occasions in the years since then, I have met remarkable non-Jews who have contributed mightily to Jewish causes. Some of them have joined protest actions that I led and displayed in the process great courage in the face of arrest and physical violence.

When I was young, I attended a yeshiva where non-Jews were spoken of with contempt. The "goyim," as non-Jews were invariably referred to, were viewed, by and large, as being out to get the Jews. From our point of view at the yeshiva, the loathing was decidedly mutual.

Many of my teachers were Holocaust survivors. Their view of the non-Jewish world had been largely shaped by that horrific experience. At the same time, they were committed to living their lives as Torah-true Jews, and the Torah speaks in powerful ethical terms about our responsibility to treat all people with dignity, respect and honor. So because of their bitter life experiences, many of my teachers struggled in their relationship with non-Jews.

I myself did not always behave in accordance with those noble precepts. In my earliest years as an activist, I was unable to imagine reaching out for support from people who were not Jewish. The teachings I had imbibed as a youth had left their mark on me. I believed that non-Jews simply could not be trusted. Fortunately, it didn't take me long to recognize how wrongheaded that outlook was. Early on in my career as an activist, and on numerous occasions in the years since then, I have met remarkable non-Jews who have contributed mightily to Jewish causes. Some of them have joined protest actions that I led and displayed in the process great courage in the face of arrest and physical violence.

I remember vividly my trip to Germany in May of 1985 to protest then-President Reagan's decision to honor the graves of those interred at a German military cemetery at Bitburg, including many Waffen SS soldiers. In an attempt to pacify an outraged American Jewish community, the President announced that while he would stick to his plan to visit the Bitburg cemetery, he would also make a stop at the one-time Nazi death camp of Bergen-Belsen in order to honor the tens of thousands of Jews who were murdered there. Yet as soon as our small group of protestors learned of Reagan's plans, we decided to travel from New York to Bergen-Belsen in order to express our abhorrence at his apparent equation of moral equivalency between murderers and victims. We were determined to make a public declaration that if Reagan went to Bitburg, he would be unwelcome at Bergen-Belsen.

With Reagan scheduled to visit Bergen-Belsen on Sunday, May 4th, we decided to arrive at the camp before the onset of Shabbat, and spend the entire Sabbath in prayer and reflection inside the gates of that terrible place—in the Bergen-Belsen Documentation Center. Our intention was to refuse the inevitable demand of the German police that we vacate the premises in advance of the President's visit. In this way we hoped to send a last minute appeal to Reagan and his handlers that they reconsider their cynical plan to use a visit to the mass graves of the Jewish victims of Bergen-Belsen as absolution for the President's subsequent obscene blessing of the tombstones of the SS men in Bitburg.

Upon arriving in Germany, I sought out members of the local Jewish community and implored my brothers and sisters to join me. Very few chose to do so. As our tiny band of protestors entered the Bergen-Belsen camp, I was dubious that we would receive any local support. Then in the midst of our Sabbath sit-in at the Bergen-Belsen Museum, three visitors approached to say they had felt spiritually uplifted observing our prayer service, and badly wanted to join our observance of Shabbat. The three were Eberhard Fiebig, his wife Dorothy, and Michael Dutching, in early middle age who had traveled to Bergen-Belsen together from the city of Kassel. Would we allow them to join us, Eberhard asked with considerable emotion, even though they were Christians and members of a nation that had behaved so horribly to the Jews? Deeply moved, I embraced each of them in turn and said we would be honored by their presence.

Eberhard was under no illusion as to the consequences of their action. He correctly predicted that the German police had decided to let us remain for the Sabbath, but would remove us immediately after Shabbat ended. Sure enough, as soon as the skies darkened, the police entered the museum and announced that the Sabbath was over and they were demanding we leave. As the cameras of the assembled television crews from around the world recorded the scene, Eberhard intoned solemnly "The Sabbath is timeless and we hereby extend it into the week."

Eberhard's tongue-in-cheek remark had the effect of giving his newfound Jewish comrades a jolt of needed energy and strength for the ordeal that lay just ahead; being removed from a Nazi death camp by German police. In effect, this was Eberhards' way of saying: "We are with you and will remain by your side no matter what." And so it was that Eberhard, his wife and friend remained with us to the end and were taken out of the museum together with us by the police. It was an unforgettable and deeply moving moment for everyone concerned; a group of Germans and

Jews standing together to protest Reagan's visit to the Bitburg Cemetery.

Here is another example of unalloyed human goodness manifested by a gentile toward Jews that I witnessed during my activist years. After John Demjanjuk returned to the United States in September of 1993, I organized a series of protest demonstrations in front of his home in Seven Hills, Ohio, a community that was predominantly Ukrainian. During the time I was leading those protests, I met with George Chandick, the mayor of Seven Hills, to inform him that although I was staunchly opposed to Demjanjuk, I had nothing against the community of Seven Hills and was not anti-Ukrainian. Although many in the community were infuriated by our demonstrations and I was probably the least popular person in town at that moment, Chandick received me in his office with respect and consideration. I was moved by his unexpected kindness at a time of great tension in the town, and at the conclusion of our meeting I stepped forward and spontaneously embraced him in front of the T.V. cameras.

Unbeknownst to me, however, Chandick was locked in a tight race for re-election. In the end, Chandick lost his re-election bid by sixteen votes. Immediately thereafter, there was a story on the front page of the *Cleveland Plain Dealer* contending that I may have cost Chandick the election by embracing him in so public a manner. Next to a photo of the two of us embracing were quotations from several Seven Hills residents stating trenchantly that they would never vote for someone who hugged a Jew.

As soon as I saw the *Plain Dealer* story, I called Chandick and told him emotionally that I had been unaware that he was in the middle of an election campaign when I hugged him and that I was saddened that anti-Semitism had cost him the election. I'll never forget his response. "Rabbi," he said, "If I had to do it again, I would do it no differently." This was one of the most profound moments of my career as an activist. Here was a non-Jew, Mayor George Chandick of Seven Hills, a predominantly Ukrainian community, declaring that even if it meant the election, he was not prepared to compromise on human dignity and honor.

Yet perhaps the moment that best illustrates for me the positive role that non-Jews can play in Jewish activism occurred in July
of 1988 outside the Mathausen death camp in Austria. Our small
group of protestors traveled to that remote spot to raise a voice of
moral conscience against Pope John Paul II, who was visiting the
camp just a day after holding his second meeting with Austrian
President Kurt Waldheim, who had been exposed several years
before as having been a Nazi war criminal during World War II.

As the Pope's helicopter landed alongside the camp, we lifted
our signs nearby, only to be jumped and manhandled by a squad
of Austrian police. They dragged us down a ravine and forced us
to stand at the edge of a forest glen. The policemen encircled us,
sneering and laughing, with their hands on their automatic
weapons. At that moment, standing there in the woods and expe-
riencing great anxiety and foreboding, I was able to experience in
a palpable way a tiny, tiny, tiny bit of the terror Jews must have
felt during the Shoah.

Suddenly, to our amazement, an elderly man came slowly
down the ravine in our direction. He approached the policemen
who were taunting us and identified himself as a professor of psy-
chology from the nearby town of Linz, before stating that he had
climbed down the steep hillside because he was concerned for our
welfare. The police tried to brush him away, telling him to leave
the area and mind his own business, but the man responded firmly that he would not budge from that spot until he knew that we
were safe. When one of the policemen demanded belligerently to
know why he was concerning himself with us, the man responded, "Too many of us looked the other way during the war. I cannot, I must not, make the same mistake."

If ever I had wondered whether the stories I had read about
Elijah the Prophet were true, those questions were answered by
that frail old man from Linz. For me, on that frightening day at
Mathausen, he himself was Elijah. At considerable risk to his own
life, Elijah stood up for Jews and declared, "I am one with you."
And by emulating the prophet of old, that Austrian, who hailed,
ironically enough, from the very town where archfiend Hitler was

raised, helped me to put forever to rest what I had been taught in my early years—that non-Jews were invariably to be distrusted and disparaged. The professor from Linz proved to me once and for all that all human beings, regardless of nationality or religion, possess the potential to manifest goodness and godliness.

March 1999

Principle Thirteen

There Must Be Ethics in Accepting Money for Activism

Charities should be more selective about their financial sources. While donors perform a *mitzvah* (good deed) in giving, recipients play no less a role in the *mitzvah* by providing the opportunity to give. In Jewish tradition, it is an honor to give. Hence, recipients have the right and obligation to develop criteria for donors.

Jewish organizations rely heavily on individual donors. Often, however, ethical dilemmas arise in regard to some contributors.

For some beneficiaries, these ethical struggles are irrelevant. After all, many agencies are so strapped for resources that they must raise massive amounts of money to survive. Establishing ethical criteria for giving may be appropriate in theoretical discussion, they claim, but without big money, worthy organizations just cannot exist. In some circles, the attitude seems to be, "Take the money; never mind where it comes from."

It shouldn't be this way. Charities should be more selective about their financial sources. While donors perform a *mitzvah* in giving, recipients play no less a role in the *mitzvah* by providing the opportunity to give. In Jewish tradition, it is an honor to give. Hence, recipients have the right and the obligation to develop criteria for donors.

It is common for most agencies to reject donations that have come from unethical endeavors. This idea accords with an age-old tradition recorded in the Talmud. The obligation to perform the *lulav* (palm) ritual on the holiday of Sukkot cannot be fulfilled with a stolen *lulav*. Rabbi Yisrael Salanter, father of the Musar movement, went even further to say, "On your way to performing a mitzvah, don't step on people."

A more difficult policy to implement is the idea that even money earned ethically should be rejected if given by someone who lives contrary to Jewish values. This principle raises the question of who, for the purpose of receiving *tzedakah*, falls into this category? Where is the line to be drawn? Spousal abuse? Intermarriage? Eating on Yom Kippur? Violating the Shabbat? Tax evasion? I believe the litmus test should be the way in which potential donors conduct their relations with others. We should leave it to God to decide who is sinning against Him, but in the area of interpersonal relationships, we must take a stand and say that we will not be party to the mistreatment of others.

Commentators ask why the patriarch Abraham preferred a wife from his birthplace for his son Isaac, rather than a woman from Canaan. After all, both were places of idolatry. Rabbeinu Nissim answers that in Canaan the people mistreated each other. In Abraham's birthplace they may have sinned against God, but there was respect and love between people. "In other words," explains the late, great biblical scholar Nehama Leibowitz, "it was not the ideas and beliefs of the family of the girl destined to be the mother of the nation that were apt to endanger the whole nation, but the evil deeds." Organizations must likewise avoid the endangering influence of contributors who harm other people.

The role benefactors play in organizational politics is also complex. On the one hand, a donor's desire to steer an agency in a particular direction is understandable. On the other hand, donors should not be allowed to become dictators. Yale University recognized this fact when it returned a twenty million dollar contribution from a benefactor who insisted that he was entitled to dictate what curriculum and which instructors would be supported by his money.

There is a related idea that is of central importance. The size of one's donation ought not be the sole criterion for leadership. Too many boards insist on large contributions as a condition for membership. It is distressing when every board member of an organization is a high-income earner and is expected to contribute large amounts. Such boards by definition do not represent the people and do not provide a place for other talents that could be of good use. Only a balance of individuals can adequately represent the community and properly assess its needs.

Of course we should never denigrate the importance of benefactors in leadership roles. The Midrash notes the partnership between Zebulon and Issachar, sons of Jacob. Zebulon was blessed with business acumen, Issachar with Torah knowledge. Although younger than his brother, Zebulon was blessed first by his father, as his finances would enable Issachar to study Torah. "Without flour," say the sages, "there is no Torah."

Those who donate must be given credit and honor; they play a critical role in the Jewish community. We must remember, however, that giving is a privilege, and a recipient of *tzedakah* also bestows an honor. There is, after all, an ethic of taking.

March 1996

Principle Fourteen

Never Trust Leaders Who Say "Trust Us"

It is fatal to allow ourselves to be patronized and rendered passive by leaders who take refuge in the "If-you-only-knew-what-we-know" refrain. The activities of our leaders must never remain secret. They must be spelled out so that the community can hold them accountable.

Once again, as thirteen Iranian Jews were being tried on trumped-up charges of espionage, denied due process, and handed severe sentences, establishment Jewish leaders have sought to lull the community into passivity with that old familiar refrain: "Trust us. If you only knew what we know. We've got the facts. We just can't share them with anyone."

We've heard that old "If-you-only-know-what-we-know" refrain before, most devastatingly during the Shoah, and we are now hearing it again. Throughout the travesty of justice inflicted on the Iranian Jews, officials of the Conference of Presidents of Major American Jewish Organizations were assuring us that they alone had the facts, and that based on those facts they alone knew exactly how to proceed. How many times do we need to hear this refrain before we wise up?

Don't worry, they assured us, we have an inside line. Don't worry, we're working behind the scenes with the U.S. government to bring sanctions against Iran. Don't worry, we've galvanized the international community through the World Bank to delay loans to Iran. Don't worry, through our intercessions the prisoners are now receiving kosher food and family visits. Don't worry, maybe a couple of the defendants will get five to six years, but most will get shorter terms.

It turns out we had a lot to worry about. It turns out that those who said they knew what was going on were almost always wrong. It turns out that instead of sanctioning Iran, the U.S. removed tariffs for Iranian goods, allowed the Iranian soccer team to visit here, and permitted Iranian diplomats to travel freely in the States. It turns out that the World Bank failed to delay the loans. It turns out that the kosher food and family visits that were allowed consisted of only one meal a week, and painfully brief visits that lasted just a few minutes. Most important, it turns out that the sentences were by no means moderate; they were extremely harsh.

The "If-you-only-knew-what-we-know" position reached its low point when the Conference insisted prior to the sentencing that public outcry would be counterproductive. To up the ante, its officials warned that they had contacts with members of the prisoners' families, *all* of whom opposed such public manifestations.

And then came the twist of the knife—our first concern must be the welfare of the prisoners, Conference leaders chided, not what makes us feel good—as if those who disagree with them don't care about the accused. To these sorts of psychological pressures can be attributed the fact that some newspapers expressed trepidation about running our ads announcing a large prayer vigil at the Iranian Mission to the U.N. The news of the trial was also effectively kept out of leading Jewish papers during the two weeks prior to the sentencing, giving the impression to the Iranian government, which closely monitors the press, that the reaction of the Jewish community was not something about which it needed to be concerned.

The fact is, family members with whom we spoke before planning our many vigils in New York gave us their blessings. Moreover, the largest prayer vigil, which attracted more than twenty-five hundred participants despite the Conference's efforts to undermine it, generated two meetings between rabbis and

Iranian officials. If public outcry has no effect, as the Conference claims, why did these officials agree to meet with us in what turned out to be the only official meeting between Jewish leaders and Iranian diplomats since the crisis began? Pooya Dayanim, a leader of the Iranian Jewish community in Los Angeles, correctly noted that the U.S. did not do more because there was no public outcry to pressure the government to be tough on Iran.

It is fatal to allow ourselves to be patronized and rendered passive by leaders who take refuge in the "If-you-only-knew-what-we-know" refrain. The activities of our leaders must never remain secret. They must be spelled out so that the community can hold them accountable. The Conference, of course, has the best interests of the accused at heart and has the right to push its own strategy, but to take the position that it is the sole authority and that its approach is the only valid one is both arrogant and dangerous. Moreover, to suggest, as some now do, that the fact that the prisoners did not receive death penalties vindicates the policy of restraint and working through backroom channels, is defeatist in the extreme. We must take absolutely no comfort at all from the harsh sentences that have been handed down.

Among those who surrendered to the behest of lay leaders condemning public protests were some of the most liberal, progressive Jews who would never tolerate following religious leaders blindly. Yet they docilely bowed to the dictates of the Conference of Presidents. The policy of blindly following was a disaster for Jews during the Shoah, and a dismal failure once again in the case of the Iranian Jews. When will we learn? The "If-you-only-knew-what-we-know" refrain is a call for complacency and powerlessness. Leaders who hide behind the "Trust-us" syndrome should never be trusted.

July 2000

Principle Fifteen

Activism Is Spiritually Encountering
Our Fellow Jews

A more appropriate term than outreach would be "encounter," which describes a mutual interaction in which all parties benefit and acquire deep respect for the other. The term also evokes how each of us, souls ignited, becomes involved in a process of continuous religious striving and, in this sense, comes to encounter our inner spiritual selves.

The guest at our Shabbat table was clearly uncomfortable wearing his *kippah*, a white bar mitzvah style skullcap that he had trouble keeping on his head. At what I thought was the proper moment, I privately handed him a knitted *yarmulke*.

He was taken aback. "I don't keep the Sabbath, I don't really deserve this gift."

"You followed along every step of the Shabbat ritual," I said. "I feel that in many ways you've become my teacher. I keep the Shabbat regularly," I continued, "but watching you, I experience it anew. You've inspired me, as very few others have, to see the beauty afresh."

The impact that this Shabbat guest and so many like him have had on people like me can be profound. When Shabbat is shared with someone who is not accustomed to observing it, it becomes, even for the most observant Jew, like a first experience. The excitement felt by the beginner is inspiring. The experienced Shabbat observer is uplifted through the spiritual joy of the learner. What might have begun as an exercise in "outreach," a term generally understood to mean that only the person "reaching out" has something to offer, is transformed into an experience from which both parties can grow. Those being reached are not viewed as having little to offer the Jewish community either spiritually or religiously; rather, outreach becomes an experience that offers a great deal to everyone involved.

Such mutuality also is true in the realm of learning. For years I've taught Bible and "Basic Jewish Concepts" to beginners. The insights of my students in these classes are often striking. My students become my teachers, sharing perceptions drawn from their experience, offering novel and creative interpretations.

The idea that outreach is a mutual experience that equally enhances both parties was cited by the first chief rabbi of Israel, Rav Avraham Yitzhak HaKohen Kook, who in the early part of the twentieth century wrote, "The souls of the observant in Torah will be perfected through the wholeness of the souls of the sinners." He went on to delineate in great detail how Orthodox Jews can learn much from the secular Zionists who were building the Jewish state.

Although it is not clear whether Rav Kook would argue today that the Orthodox can learn from the non-Orthodox in the same manner as when he articulated this idea almost a hundred years ago, he does lay down the important principle that observant Jews can derive much from the less observant. What can be learned varies from generation to generation.

In addition to the mutuality inherent in outreach at its best, there is yet another aspect of outreach that needs to be reconsidered. Success in outreach too often is defined as managing to convince other Jews to become fully committed. This should not be so. There is a middle ground. If the one to whom we reach out is influenced to feel a greater commitment to the Jewish people, or if he or she decides to observe only certain parts of the Shabbat or the dietary laws, or if our contact represents a beginning that yields results even in the next generation, these steps too constitute success.

"It's not for you to complete the task," says Rabbi Tarphon, "but neither are you excused from undertaking it." The most lasting religious growth is gradual, a process rather than a radical transformation.

Our understanding of the concept and practice of outreach must be refined in two crucial ways.

First, those doing the outreach must realize that they have much to learn from those being reached.

Second, the goal of outreach is to inspire not only the observance of ritual but also the stirring of Jewish consciousness, the lighting of a spiritual fire that allows those being touched to chart their own direction.

For these reasons a more appropriate term than outreach would be "encounter," which describes a mutual interaction in which all parties benefit and acquire deep respect for the other. The term also evokes how each of us, souls ignited, becomes involved in a process of continuous religious striving and, in this sense, comes to encounter our inner spiritual selves.

It should be noted too that such encounters need not be the exclusive province of rabbis, national organizations, or other officials, but rather is an activity in which every Jew can individually engage.

Each of us ought to ask, When was the last time a less observant Jew was at my Shabbat table? When was the last time I studied Torah with a less observant Jew? When was the last time I sat near a less observant Jew in shul? If we can't answer these questions, then why not enrich our lives by resolving to start "encountering" this coming Shabbat.

October 1997

DESIGNING THE STRATEGY

The Spiritual Activist recognizes that it is necessary to understand the practical aspects of how public protest works.

The Spiritual Activist knows how to deal with the media, how to understate the facts, how to be single-minded and relentless, and how to strike while the iron is hot before it is too late.

The Spiritual Activist accepts the occasional need for strident action—for going into the lion's den—but only as a last resort and never accompanied by violence.

The Spiritual Activist creates and supports centers of spirituality.

Principle Sixteen

Understand How Public Protest Works

Public protest not only sends a message to the victimizers that the eyes of the world are watching, but it also inspires governments around the world to exert pressure in order to put an end to the outrage. Not to be underestimated is the effect public expressions of solidarity have on the beleaguered, who, as a result of such actions understand and feel that they are not alone.

Amir Zamaninia, consul of the Iranian Mission to the U.N., was as cordial as could be as he offered a spirited defense last week of his country's trial of thirteen Jews accused of espionage to Rabbi Abe Cooper of the Simon Wiesenthal Center and to me.

Mr. Zamaninia's willingness to consent to a meeting took us by surprise. As part of our preparations for a prayer vigil on behalf of the Iran Thirteen, we faxed a letter to the Iranian Mission requesting that a delegation of rabbis be permitted to present its concerns to Iranian officials. Within hours our request was answered and the next morning the precise time was set.

The meeting was the first to take place between U.S. Jewish leaders and Iranian officials since the arrest of thirteen Iranian Jews sixteen months ago on charges of spying for Israel. Apparently, all previous official attempts to sit down face to face with Iranian representatives had been rebuffed.

No doubt the Iranian U.N. Mission staff had not independently made the decision to convene the meeting. Orders came from authorities in Teheran who could not ignore announcements of the prayer vigil in the press and on several area radio stations.

But during the week prior to the vigil, the Conference of Presidents of Major American Jewish Organizations did its best to sabotage our efforts. This Jewish establishment group claimed that a prayer vigil convened as the trial drew to a close would have no impact since Iran was impervious to public outcry. Conference officials argued that the vigil would ignite a backlash in Iran and precipitate protests against Jews living in Shiraz.

As we sat in Mr. Zamaninia's office, it was clear that the reverse was true. If the Iranians were impervious to world public opinion, why would they bother to meet with us? Why offer a spirited defense of the proceedings to American Jews if they didn't care about our reaction?

The Conference of Presidents assured American Jewry that it was working quietly behind the scenes to effect sanctions against Iran, specifically through delays in granting Iran significant loans from the World Bank. But in the days before the prayer vigil took place, the loans were given the go-ahead. Even the Conference of Presidents' assertion that the families of those jailed preferred that there be no public outcry proved to be incorrect. I spoke with family members who gave us their blessings for the dignified public prayer on behalf of their relatives.

During the Holocaust, the Jewish community relied on a select group of individuals who maintained that it was privy to facts it could not share with anyone. Even so, these individuals demanded the trust of the Jewish community. Germany is impervious to protest, they argued, and therefore, public outcry would be counterproductive. Their motives are not to be questioned, but in the end they were wrong.

In the case of Iran, public protest not only sends a message that the eyes of the world are watching, but it also inspires governments around the world to pressure Iran to put an end to this outrage. Today, America is prepared to allow Iranian soccer teams to visit the U.S.; it has allowed Iranian officials to travel across the

U.S., despite Iran's presence on the State Department's list of terrorist countries; and it is negotiating to restore diplomatic ties with Iran. Only through public outcry can we emphasize to our government that relations with Iran must be based on the pillars of human rights.

Not to be underestimated is the effect public expressions of solidarity have on those in jail, who, as a result of such actions, understand and feel that they are not alone. The recent recanting of a confession implicating his brother by one of the accused is, we are convinced, due to a greater awareness that people in the West really care.

Sitting in his office as the crowds gathered on the streets below for what would prove to be—despite the undermining attempts of the Conference of Presidents—the largest outpouring of solidarity with the Iran Thirteen, the consul wanted to know why we were protesting the trial before it was concluded. Rabbi Cooper and I responded that the proceedings themselves, carried on behind closed doors, with the prosecutor and judge one and the same person, are fundamentally flawed. Mr. Zamaninia countered that even in the U.S., a trial that involves national security issues, such as that of Jonathan Pollard, is closed. We informed him that the Pollard case never even went to trial. Mr. Zamaninia's next tactic was to claim that open trials would cause problems for Jews in Iran. Why then, we asked, did the Iranian government allow the confessions of the accused to be aired on Iranian national TV?

Mr. Zamaninia continued to defend his government's actions even as we rose to leave to begin the prayer vigil. Expressing appreciation for his time, Rabbi Cooper handed a letter to the consul asking permission for a small delegation of rabbis to visit the prisoners in Shiraz.

The fact that this meeting even took place proves once and for all that Iran is exquisitely sensitive to western public opinion. It underscores the truth that public protest protects the oppressed, and enhances the voice of those engaged in quiet diplomacy.

May 2000

Principle Seventeen

Deal Honestly with the Media

The media, notwithstanding its importance in getting the message across, should never be deceived even in ways that may appear relatively benign. . . . A critical test of activism is the readiness to be out there whether the cameras are present or not; whether the media believes our issue is important or not. It should always be remembered that media coverage is a tool of activism and not its goal.

It has happened so many times. A television crew arrives late to one of our demonstrations and asks us to repeat for their cameras the protest action we have just concluded. Obediently, we go through the motions again. Each time I wonder, Are we correct in performing such a charade, participating in a deception? After all, viewers of the evening news will believe that they are seeing a live protest, when in reality they are watching a canned event created especially for the cameras. There was a time during my activist career when I believed that all was fair vis-à-vis the media. The cause was paramount, and therefore the ends always justified the means.

The Torah, however, instructs us differently. *Tzedek, tzedek tirdof,* "justice, justice you shall pursue." Why the repetition of the term *tzedek*? the commentators ask. Dr. Samuel Belkin answered the question by translating the text as "justice you shall justly pursue." In other words, the end, no matter how noble, does not justify the use of ignoble means.

This moral paradigm holds true in the world of activism. Among my ground rules for honorable activism are that violence should never be used as a means to promote social change; that protest organizers should never take demonstrators by surprise—for example, no one should be manipulated into giving the appearance of supporting actions of which they disapprove; and that the media, notwithstanding its importance in getting the message across, should never be deceived, even in ways that may appear relatively benign.

I do not mean to suggest that activists should eschew the opportunity to use the media honorably to get their message out. Hubert Humphrey once said that, when giving a speech, he always spoke to the cameras, an honest expression of standard operating procedure for politicians. After all, through the media the message will go far beyond the crowd at hand. No matter how large the assemblage, many more will be reached through the press. It should be remembered that the amount of people present at a rally may not necessarily be important to the media. Over and over I have seen how a few people have had their "action" broadcast to the world—sometimes impacting powerfully on a particular issue. Size doesn't always matter.

From this perspective, packaging a sound bite as best one can, using appropriate props, and planning a dramatic protest action the day before a major affair of state in the awareness that the journalists will be hungry for something to report in the run-up to the main event—these are all honest techniques that fall within the range of the acceptable.

Dealing honestly with the media does not mean that representatives of the media will necessarily act forthrightly toward us. Journalism, like any other profession, is made up of individuals, some good, some not, some honest, some not. Some reporters are diligent while others are sloppy. All too often, I come across reporters whose subjective feelings about a story influence their reporting. Yet even if the media portrays the activist inaccurately, the activist should always remain truthful.

As we remain truthful, we must recognize that the media is so powerful that it sometimes can lure us into altering what is the very soul of activism.

For example, as activists, we must be very wary of any tendency toward fashioning our agenda to reflect what we expect the media will find attractive. A critical test of activism is the readiness to be out there whether the cameras are present or not, whether the media believes our issue is important or not. It should always be remembered that media coverage is a tool of activism but not its goal. In fact, at an event, activists should conduct themselves as if the media were not there. Playing to the cameras can alter the activist's sense of purity of mission. The overriding concern could become how he or she will be portrayed on TV or in the newspapers. If we allow that to occur, we run the risk of blurring the goals and meaning of an action. Ironically, I have found that more favorable coverage is given when—contrary to Hubert Humphrey's assertion—activists address themselves to the crowd, not to the media. As a general rule then, one should focus on the action at hand, not on the reporters covering the action.

Another example: There was a time, not so long ago, when activism generated the participation of hundreds of thousands who gathered throughout the world in protest on behalf of Soviet Jewry. Activism then was plainly the expression of the *amcha*. Today activism is often played out in advertisements, especially in newspapers. This practice has too often relegated activism to the wealthy, more elitist organizations who have the means to buy ad space but whose ads may not reflect the agenda, needs, and goals of the grassroots community. Moreover, these ads give what cumulatively could be millions of dollars to papers that are anti-Israel, and in the process dramatically increase the prestige of these papers.

So were we right when we played our protest over for TV crews that arrived late? For the evening's news cycle, maybe we came out ahead. Yet over time, such gains prove ephemeral.

An activist planning to advance a cause over the long haul must reject the temptation to indulge in ethical shortcuts. Dr. Belkin's standard should be applied across the board: "Justice thou shall justly pursue."

July 1996

Principle Eighteen

Understate the Facts

Caught up in a particular cause, advocates may be tempted to overstate their case. Those who do so are advised to remember that those who speak "loudest" are not necessarily heard best. One should be so careful to make sure one is honestly and fully putting forth the facts, that when in doubt about a particular point, one should speak in even more moderate and measured tones. Far from weakening one's position, the soft voice, the reasoned voice, the understated voice is the more believable voice.

An oft-repeated rabbinical joke concerns a rabbi who carefully prepares a sermon, writing it out word for word. Reading it over, he notes a particular idea that seems forced. Despite intense effort to strengthen the thought, he finds himself unable to do so. Finally, in exasperation, he jots down in the margin, "Weak point, speak loud!" And when he realizes that the next paragraph is similarly flawed, he writes, "Weaker still, speak louder."

While the rabbi may hope that raising his voice will balance out the weakness of his argument, his audience is not likely to be fooled. In fact, the higher the decibel of the oratory, the less inclined people will be to listen, and the more suspicious the audience will become about the veracity of the ideas being presented.

In truth, speaking loud is not only about raising the volume of one's voice. Sometimes a person can speak softly but use words so exaggerated or hyperbolic that the effect is the same as if they had been screamed from the rooftops. The listener first becomes skeptical and soon is downright suspicious, wondering whether such fantastic claims can really be true. Despite, or perhaps because of, the barrage of slick arguments and wild claims put forth by Madison Avenue and too many of our political leaders, the public has developed an uncanny instinct for detecting untruths. One attribute of that instinct is the ability to recognize overstatements and to dismiss them as attempts to compensate for flawed arguments.

If a leader who chronically exaggerates loses credibility, an even direr possible consequence is that the audience might actually believe those words to be true. Consider the biblical report of the men sent out by Moses to scout the land of Israel. One can make the case that their mistake lay not in reporting that the land would be difficult to conquer, but rather in their inflated phraseology. The inhabitants, they reported, were giants and we looked like grasshoppers in comparison. The Israelites believed the report to be the literal truth and rebelled. In the end, thousands were killed and the generation that left Egypt was doomed to die in the desert.

There is another danger in overstating. If the advocate is caught up in even what amounts to a small lie or a shading of the truth, then the overall position being put forth—which may in fact be true—is called into question.

The Midrash makes this point when it suggests that Eve made a mistake when she told the snake in the Garden of Eden that God had forbidden the touching of the tree of knowledge, when in fact God had only prohibited the eating of its fruits. In the words of the Midrash, the snake pushed Eve against the tree and said slyly, "As nothing happened when you touched it, so nothing will happen if you eat of it." The Midrash concludes, "She added to the commandment; therefore she came to diminish from it."

Here is another, more contemporary case in point. Jonathan Pollard is the victim of a grave injustice. Nonetheless it is a mistake for his supporters to overreach in their advocacy on his behalf by

comparing his case to the Dreyfus Affair or to the long imprisonment of Natan Sharansky by Soviet authorities. Why so? The truth
of the matter is that while Dreyfus and Sharansky were innocent
of the crimes with which they were charged, Pollard was in fact
guilty of spying on behalf of Israel. Once the previously unin-
formed listener is apprised of the falseness of the comparison
between Pollard on one hand and Dreyfus and Sharansky on the
other, he or she may also conclude that the most compelling and
irrefutable aspect of Pollard's argument—namely, that he is a victim of wildly excessive punishment—is similarly flawed.
Therefore, those who make false or exaggerated claims on
Pollard's behalf are undermining the chances for release from
prison that he fully deserves.

It is also the case, of course, that overstating the facts flies in the
face of Torah law which demands that we be honest. In fact, we are
advised to remain far from anything that appears to be untruthful,
far from what the Talmud calls the "dust of dishonesty." For the
Talmud, this category includes not only uttering a falsehood, but
even remaining silent when our silence gives the false impression
that we are prepared to offer testimony on a particular issue.

Passionately caught up in a particular cause, advocates are
tempted to overstate their case. Those who do so are advised to
pay heed to the parable of the rabbi who deluded himself into
believing that he could drive home his points by shouting. The
truth is that those who speak loudest are not necessarily heard
best. One should be so careful to ensure that one is putting forth
the facts honestly and fully, that when in doubt about a particular
point, one should speak in even more moderate and nuanced
tones. Far from weakening one's position, the soft voice, the reasoned voice, the understated voice is the more believable voice.

May 1999

Principle Nineteen

Learn the Power of Tenacity

Activism that yields quick results is relatively easy—exciting, stimulating, fulfilling. It is, however, most often the case, that change does not happen overnight. It comes, rather, in gradual, almost indiscernible increments. In fact, the Talmud talks about the short path that turns out to be long and the long path that ends up being short. Even when things progress slowly, results can come, and sometimes they are more lasting.

My dear friend, the late Dr. Charles Kremer was a Romanian born dentist who dedicated his life to pursuing Valerian D. Trifa, the former head of the Nazi Iron Guard in Romania. In December 1941, Trifa led a pogrom in Bucharest during which two hundred Jews had their throats cut inside the city slaughterhouse. The bodies of the Jews were hung from meathooks, and signs reading "kosher meat" were placed on each of the victim's chests.

In 1949, Trifa illegally entered the United States, violating U.S. law prohibiting the immigration of anyone with a Nazi past. Incredibly, several years after his arrival, Trifa managed to have himself consecrated as Archbishop of the Romanian Orthodox Church of America. He was then appointed to the executive committee of the prestigious National Council of Churches, an umbrella organization of thirty-one Christian groups that represented forty-two million people. On one occasion in the 1950s, this foul mass-murderer was given the honor of reciting the opening prayer at a session of the U.S. House of Representatives.

Yet despite Trifa's high standing, Dr. Kremer, a resident of Philadelphia who had lost members of his own family at the hands of the Iron Guard, doggedly persisted in a lonely and seemingly impossible battle to have the archbishop stripped of his citizenship and deported from the United States. Closing his dental practice in the early 1950s in order to devote himself full-time to his mission, Dr. Kremer traveled to Romania and Israel at his own expense, meticulously sifting through reams of yellowing documents and interviewing scores of survivors of the Bucharest pogrom. Eventually the indomitable ex-dentist amassed a mountain of evidence proving Trifa's role in precipitating the Bucharest massacre. This evidence was so compelling that even the U.S. Immigration and Naturalization Service, which had earlier cleared the archbishop of wrongdoing, could no longer go on insisting that Trifa was innocent.

For me it was Dr. Kremer's extraordinary tenacity that distinguished him from other activists. His work did not yield immediate results—it took him thirty-five years to win his fight. Yet even when it appeared that he was making no progress, he never gave up.

The idea that persistence is a necessary trait for successful activism runs counter to the common understanding of the nature of activism, which is often associated in the public mind with precipitous change. During our decades-long campaign to save Soviet Jewry, I received countless calls from participants in our demonstrations who complained, "I was out there, so how come they are still not free?"

The presumption that an action precipitates immediate metamorphosis is part of the American psyche. In America, speed is paramount, and what's "in" is what's fast, whether it's food, computers, news stories, or making an instant "killing" on the stock market. But it is not always the case that things happen quickly.

This message can be found in the biblical narrative. Abraham and Sarah waited twenty-five years for a child; Jacob lived for no fewer than twenty-two years in the hope that Joseph would return; while the Jews yearned for redemption from Egypt for over two hundred years.

Rabbi Akiva, the Talmud tells us, began to study at the age of forty. Feeling frustrated because he felt he wasn't learning fast enough, he once noticed water dripping slowly onto a rock. The rock was slightly indented. Akiva thought, "Just as it took the water years and years to make a mark, so too will I gradually amass Torah knowledge." So it was.

Dr. Samuel Belkin makes a similar point. Commenting on the rabbinical dictum that "all beginnings are difficult," he asked, why "beginnings" in the plural and not in the singular? Dr. Belkin responded that the axiom teaches that each venture may have more than one beginning. It requires steadfastness to start over and over again.

It is often the tactic of those who are stronger, wealthier, more influential, and more established to endeavor to wear the activist down. That was the successful strategy employed by the U.S. government against family members of the victims of Pan Am flight #103, which blew up over Scotland in 1988. Many of the family members, with whom I joined in coordinating protests, remain convinced that Syria played a major role in the plot to bring the plane down. They are infuriated that their own government mendaciously shifted all of the blame for the crash to Libya in order to protect the image of the Syrians, who were being touted by Washington as partners in the Middle East peace process. Over time, most of the family members have given up their struggle to force the State Department to reveal the truth. As the years go by, good people often get tired and drop out as the relentless power of government overwhelms them.

While I understand the plight of those personally victimized who, worn out by anguish and exhaustion, cannot go on, those who have not been directly affected should never give up the battle. With tenacity, activists can overcome all the formidable obstacles confronting them if they hold on to the rabbinical maxim that "nothing can stand in the face of the will." This means being out there not only for the first time, but following through even when facing obstacles. It means being present even when the cameras are not. It means remaining fired up and committed to the cause even when one is marginalized by officials—whether by the government or by the more established advocacy groups—who insist that the issue is a non-issue.

Activism that yields quick results is relatively easy—exciting, stimulating, fulfilling. It is most often the case, however, that change does not happen overnight. It comes rather in gradual, almost indiscernible increments. In fact, the Talmud talks about the short path that turns out to be long, and the long path that ends up being short. Even when things progress slowly, results can come and sometimes these are more lasting.

I'll never forget when Trifa was finally denaturalized and deported. "I finally got the bastard," my friend Dr. Charles Kremer declared triumphantly.

He did, but only because he knew the power of tenacity.

April 1997

Principle Twenty

Be There on Time

Often a cause is clearly right and quite simply cries out for support, and yet even the most well intentioned and highly motivated person may be prone to procrastination. "Yes," the activist thinks, "this issue is important but I am extremely busy with other pressing matters right now. I'll get involved tomorrow." The problem is, all too often, tomorrow never comes. Timing—including making sure that we get there on time—is every bit as important as the act of becoming involved.

Sometimes I wonder whether or not the present really exists. We seem so caught up in planning for the future and reminiscing about the past that we can't seem to find the time to experience the present. We prepare so intensely for a particular moment in the future, and then, as quickly as it arrives in the present, it disappears—an instant buried in the past.

This is not the case in the world of Judaism. Rabbi Israel Lipshutz, a medieval Jewish commentator, points out that given that God is above and beyond time, He experiences both the human past, present and future all at once. In the spirit of *imitatio dei*, we who are created in God's image, although living in a particular time, should accentuate the convergence of past and future in the here and now.

Not coincidentally, the word *"hayom"* (today) is emphasized in the Bible. In fact, it appears in the last five portions of the Torah.

These readings are recited in the weeks before and after the High Holy Day, reminding us of the importance of "today."

The concept of "*hayom*" also takes on special significance in the world of spiritual activism. Often a cause is clearly right and quite simply cries out for support, and yet even the most well intentioned and highly motivated person may be prone to procrastination. "Yes," the activist thinks, "this issue is important but I am extremely busy with other pressing matters right now. I'll get involved tomorrow." The problem is, all too often, tomorrow never comes. Timing—including making sure that we get there on time—is every bit as important as the act of becoming involved.

Several years ago, the tragic bombing of the AMIA Jewish Community Center in Buenos Aires presented me with the opportunity to confront the tendency to procrastinate. The moment I saw the horrific scenes on television, I knew I had to go there immediately—not the next day, but that very day. I arrived in the Argentine capital in time to witness the victims still being dug out from under the rubble, and to comfort the families of those who had been senselessly killed while the stench of human remains still fouled the air. I pray that my presence in Buenos Aires sent an important message to the shell-shocked and grief-stricken Argentine Jewish community: that world Jewry cared for them and was there to help.

I left Buenos Aires grateful that I had not delayed in making the trip. One of the basic principles of spiritual activism is—go! While watching the first horrifying televised images of the explosion on CNN, I wondered, "Does it pay to travel to Argentina? I don't speak the language, I know few people there." Yet once I set forth on that trip, I found out, as I have discovered repeatedly on other activist travels, that once I commit myself to going and get on board the plane, things fall rapidly into place. In fact, of all the many trips I have made as an activist, the one to Buenos Aires proved to be the most fulfilling. I found that I was able to combine my roles as rabbi, activist and humanitarian all at once.

I have learned over the years as an activist that it is often the case that responding quickly, even if it means a smaller number of people will be at a particular demonstration or event, is more effective than waiting in order to organize greater participation. Proper timing is an essential ingredient for successful spiritual activism.

The group of commandments circumscribed by time teach us this very idea. Not coincidentally, the first mitzvah given to the Jewish people in the Torah is to count in accordance with the lunar year. And the first law found in the Talmud concerning the times of day when the *Shema* is to be recited, also deals with time.

One interpretation of the "Binding of Isaac" narrative also reinforces this concept. Several years ago, as I was studying with my students the sentences that vividly describe how Abraham lifted his knife to kill his son Isaac, I realized that in recent years, I have come to view this narrative from the perspective of being a grandfather. Each time I read it, I feel fear and anguish for the life of Isaac, seeing in my mind's eye any of my own grandchildren in his place.

I explained to my students that two concurrent scenes unfold in the story. First, as Abraham stands there gripping the knife, his hand moves downward toward Isaac's neck. Almost simultaneously, an angel descends to warn Abraham not to kill his son. Though I've read this text hundreds of times and know the outcome, whenever I read it anew, I have a moment of fear as to whether the angel will get there on time.

Filled with genuine emotion from reading the story with my students, I concluded that the message of the text is that the angel arrived just in the nick of time. It is surely one of the most heart-stopping, suspenseful scenes in the entire Bible.

Yet more recently, Rabbi David Saperstein pointed out to me that Rabbi Abraham Joshua Heschel once remarked concerning the Binding of Isaac story, "While angels always get there on time, people don't."

Heschel's message is clear. When challenges present themselves, it is crucial for the spiritual activist to go and to be there on time. Paraphrasing the words of the sage, "Do not say when I will have time, I will do, as that time may never come."

No wonder we conclude the services on the morning of Rosh Hashanah with the joyous song, "*Hayom*." The irony is that on the day of Rosh Hashanah, when we celebrate the opportunity to repent, in effect acknowledging the privilege of being given a second chance in the future, we declare "*hayom*." Sometimes the only chance is today, and if it's missed, the opportunity is lost forever.

The popular songs, "Yesterday" and "Tomorrow," are poignant, even beautiful, but for the spiritual activist, the most meaningful song is "Today." Yesterday is behind us and tomorrow may be too late.

January 1999

Principle Twenty-One

Go Into the Lion's Den

As a matter of principle, the further away you are from the scene of controversy, the less potent the protest. Conversely, the closer you are, the more dramatic the protest. And as centuries of theater attest, the best drama is powerful and demands attention.

Invariably, when my activist colleagues and I engage in direct-action protests, we are criticized. "I agree with your goals," people say, "but why are you so confrontational? Sit back and allow more civil discourse to take place."

In most situations, it is true, civil discourse or quiet diplomacy has a place. However, it is direct action—going to the point of tension—that complements quiet diplomacy and often is the most effective response.

As a matter of principle, the further away you are from the scene of controversy, the less potent the protest. Conversely, the closer you are, the more dramatic the protest. And as centuries of theater attest, the best drama is powerful and demands attention.

For example, in December 1991, as David Duke announced his presidential candidacy at the National Press Club, I held up a sign in the back of the crowded room. This action had virtually no impact. It was only when I was able to maneuver the sign just inches from his face that the drama, the action, the attention followed suit. That was the picture that went around the country: David Duke right beside a sign that read, "Duke Is the Nazi of the '90s."

The message was carried clearly only because of my proximity to Duke himself.

Furthermore, direct action frequently has the effect of unmasking insincerity, falsehood, and bigotry. No matter how outrageous his position, the most virulent racist in this media-conscious era is able to memorize sound bites that project an image of kindness and fair play. Direct intervention can sometimes catch the person off guard, forcing him to react spontaneously in ways that reveal his true character. The real test of a human being, say the rabbis, is how a person reacts when angered.

For example, when following Pat Buchanan around the country during the 1992 and 1996 presidential campaigns, my colleagues and I always tried to stage our protest as close as possible to the would-be candidate. On the eve of the Georgia primary in March 1992 I stood with other rabbis only a few inches from Buchanan. As the candidate pounded away at his "America First" theme, I called out, "You anti-Semitism makes America last!" Buchanan shot back, clearly forgetting to filter and censor himself, "This is a rally of Americans, for Americans and for the good old USA, my friends." Buchanan's mask was gone.

When provoked, his true sentiments were revealed: Jews and others who disagree with him are not real Americans. Even the usually cautious American Jewish Congress was moved to declare: "There has been much public speculation about Pat Buchanan's true feelings about Jews; this time he has removed all doubt. Pat Buchanan is as genuine and authentic an anti-Semite as they come."

Here then is another benefit that emerges from direct action: Once the issue has been dramatized and the essence of the person being protested is revealed, those who had heretofore remained on the sidelines are forced into discomfort with their own passivity and are moved to take a position.

This point was further emphasized by the Riverdale Press in an editorial after our demonstration at the Auschwitz convent in July 1989 and Poland's Cardinal Glemp's assertion that we had come to destroy the convent and kill the nuns: "This protest demonstrated, as no polite appeal could, how deeply ingrained the condition that permitted the murder of millions remains. The sit-down at the convent stripped away the mask of official contrition. In his denunciatory address Cardinal Glemp disclosed what lay beneath. In accomplishing this unmasking, the demonstrators transcended the issue of the convent. . . . They forced people everywhere to stir from their passivity to choose sides, to proclaim what is right."

Despite all the benefits of direct action, the protester is vulnerable to the criticism of being an outsider who doesn't belong. Virtually everywhere we've gone—in Argentina, Turkey, Poland, Austria, even in the United States—we've been criticized by local Jewish leadership for intervening in issues that they claim are not our business.

As a student of the social activism of Dr. Martin Luther King, Jr., I have for a long time been in a position to understand and remind others of his response to such charges. When White clergy in Birmingham, Alabama, criticized Dr. King, calling him an outsider, he replied, "I am in Birmingham because injustice is here." That is a response we should all heed closely: To act peacefully, powerfully at the point of tension, even if doing so means going into the lion's den.

January 1997

Principle Twenty-Two

Strident Action Should Be an Instrument of Last Resort

An essential principle of activism is that strident demonstrations should not be the first steps taken when trying to combat a specific injustice. Rather, attention-getting civil disobedience ought to be the final step—one that should be taken only after quieter and less polarizing forms of protests have been exhausted, and only after careful consideration has been given to the possible consequences of stepping dramatically into the breach.

When we peacefully demonstrated against the Carmelite convent at the Auschwitz death camp in July 1989 by climbing over the gate and surrounding the building—an action that led to our being badly beaten by a group of Polish workers—some in the American Jewish establishment responded to this anti-Semitic outrage by choosing to blame the victims, labeling us "extremists."

Six years later several of us were arrested in Auschwitz-Birkenau. This time our "crime" consisted of conducting a sit-in at a church which had been established in 1983 in a building that had once served as the headquarters of the Nazi commandant in Birkenau, which was the actual theater of death in Auschwitz. It was in Birkenau, rather than in the better-known Auschwitz I section of the vast hellish complex, where 1.1 million Jews were incinerated. We were taken to the Auschwitz police station and subjected to a terrible humiliation when the Polish police forced us to strip to the waist. Despite all this, our action was once again condemned by leaders, who dismissed us as publicity-seeking provocateurs.

I take deep exception to these charges. One should not rush to the point of maximum tension at the drop of a hat whenever one feels that the honor of one's people has been impugned. Far from it. An essential principle of the activism I espouse is that demonstrations of the type we conducted at the convent and church in Auschwitz-Birkenau should not be the first steps taken in trying to combat a specific injustice. Rather, attention-grabbing civil disobedience of that type ought to be the final step, taken only after quieter and less polarizing forms of protest have been exhausted, and only after careful consideration has been given to the possible consequences of stepping dramatically into the breach.

In the case of the Auschwitz convent, we did not jump thoughtlessly into the fray as soon as the existence of the convent at the death camp became a cause célèbre in the Jewish community. The fact is that by the time we moved, world Jewry had been protesting to the Vatican for years about the presence of the convent in Auschwitz. Two years earlier four European cardinals and a group of European Jewish leaders had signed a "solemn agreement" promising that the Carmelite nuns at the Auschwitz convent would move out of the building by January 22, 1989. That date came and went. The nuns declared defiantly that they would never leave Auschwitz, and there was little response from the Vatican besides an ineffectual wringing of hands. We waited six months beyond the deadline but nothing happened and there seemed little prospect that further "quiet diplomacy" was going to move the recalcitrant nuns. It was only at that juncture that we traveled to Poland and climbed over the fence at the Auschwitz convent.

We took similar pains in the case of our protest at the Birkenau church six years later, resolving not to move before other avenues had been exhausted. It was crystal clear that the presence of the church in Birkenau was in flagrant violation of the same 1987 agreement reached between the cardinals and European Jewish leaders, which declared clearly that "There shall be no permanent place of worship at Auschwitz-Birkenau." That proviso seemed ironclad, but there was a curious lack of will on the part of the Vatican and the Polish church to make sure the agreement was honored. Only after issuing countless fruitless demands that the church relocate from the former death camp did we finally board the plane to Poland to embark on our sit-in at the Birkenau church.

The Torah portion that deals with the Exodus from Egypt—the paradigmatic narrative for activism—makes clear that the ten plagues were inflicted by God upon the Egyptians only after Pharaoh ignored countless warnings to free the Jews. In fact some commentators view the first nine plagues as being divided into three, with the first two plagues of each trio not affecting the "body" of the Egyptians but only their environment. For example, the plague of blood attacked the water outside the home, frogs entered the home, and then and only then did lice actually attack the Egyptian people. According to these commentators, the first two plagues in each trio amounted to stern warnings to Pharaoh, and only after they were ignored was a more devastating directly personal plague unleashed.

The message conveyed here is that God acts decisively only after less onerous actions prove futile. Thus we learn that strident action should only be an instrument of last resort.

This principle applies to virtually all areas of concern. Consider the plight of the *agunah*, the woman whose husband denies her a *get*, the Jewish bill of divorce. Here it is necessary for the Jewish community to impose sanctions against a husband in order to force him to give the *get*. Those pressures can go as far as holding protest demonstrations in front of the husband's place of business or home and denying him entry into synagogue. But other steps must be taken first, such as demanding the *get*, warning the husband of the consequences of not giving it, mentioning the husband's name publicly in the synagogue, or even taking out ads in the local papers denouncing his recalcitrance. When these steps have been tried and proven futile direct action becomes necessary.

In fact, not only should direct, strident action be the last step, but activists ought to remember that the threat is sometimes more potent than the act of itself. There is a story of a rebbe who, after his death, visits his favorite student in a dream and glowingly describes to his protégé the beauty of the next world. "Would you even consider coming back to this world?" the student asked. "Oh no," said the rebbe. "The fear of dying is too much to handle."

Here is an instance illustrative of that point. Prior to the fiftieth anniversary of the Warsaw Ghetto uprising in January 1993, which was to be commemorated by the Polish government and world Jewry with a solemn observance in the Polish capital, the Coalition for Jewish Concerns/*Amcha* announced that we would again travel to Auschwitz to protest outside the convent unless the nuns fulfilled the repeated promises of the Vatican and moved out. Just days before Israeli Prime Minister Yitzhak Rabin was to arrive in Warsaw to take part in the commemoration, Pope John Paul II finally put his foot down after years of vacillating and gave the nuns a stern order to evacuate immediately.

Asked by the *New York Times* what precipitated the Pope's decision, Konstatin Gebert, an influential Polish Jewish leader, said, "The threat of protest left the [Polish] government with no choice." Gebert meant that as a result of our threatened protest, the Polish government had no choice but to see the nuns moved if they wanted to prevent the carefully planned Warsaw Ghetto event from dissolving into bitter recriminations; evidently it appealed to the Vatican with an S.O.S. to that effect. Soon after, the stubborn nuns, who had hitherto held the fort in the Auschwitz convent for some eight years, were finally gone.

The requirement that activists allow time before engaging in civil disobedience does not foreclose less strident public protest as an early on option. And if strident action becomes necesary it need not be limited to aggressive demonstrations. One can use the legal and political system in a strident manner as well, like when we sued Howard University for violating our right to protest against Khalid Abdul Muhammad's many appearances on its campus. Another example is when we successfully lobbied the House International Affairs Committee to convene hearings on why the

Argentine government of Carlos Menem had done little to capture the terrorists responsible for blowing up the Israeli embassy and the AMIA Jewish community center in Buenos Aires.

Truth be told, our community has long focused its energy on reaching cozy, behind-the-scenes understandings within the corridors of power. This mode of operation has sometimes been effective, but the deft application of money and power alone are not enough.

We must therefore be prepared to raise a voice of conscience, even at the cost of angering those in powerful positions. By emulating the philosophy and tactics of nonviolent protest espoused by Dr. Martin Luther King, Jr., we can succeed in elucidating for our fellow citizens the moral passion for truth and justice behind the positions we advocate.

When we demonstrate, however, we ought always do so with forethought. Strident action and civil disobedience are powerful tools with profound consequences and should be used only when appropriate and only when other means are exhausted. That was the case during our protest actions at the Auschwitz convent and at the Birkenau church. In both cases, we had reached an impasse with those who sought to Christianize the largest Jewish graveyard in the world in order to erase awareness of the Jewishness of those who were murdered there. We had no choice but to do what we did. The waters had already reached the collective neck of our people.

November 1999

Principle Twenty-Three

Reject Violence as a Means of Social Action

Once individuals assume the right to defend themselves with arms as a means of social action, they open the Pandora's box for other, more random acts of violence. The distance between legitimate and illegitimate acts of violence is a hair's breadth.

In the early years of my activism I was inspired by Rabbi Meir Kahane. Here was a proud Jew, I thought, who would not tolerate a repetition of the passivity of the American Jewish community during the Holocaust. Rabbi Kahane's talks were fiery. He kept his audience spellbound as he spoke of the biblical incident of the Egyptian smiting the Jew. Moses looked around, saw that no one cared, Rabbi Kahane said, and he knew what to do—he smote the Egyptian. What would the establishment have done? No doubt they would have called for a committee meeting. Moses, Rabbi Kahane concluded, taught us that there should be an eleventh commandment: Thou shalt not committ—ee.

Rabbi Kahane believed that violence was a crucial element in defending Jews around the world. During the early years of the Soviet Jewry movement, he insisted that only violent protests could garner the media attention necessary to lead to freedom for Soviet Jews. This position was one I always opposed. Even in the early days when I was attracted to Rabbi Kahane's philosophy, the Student Struggle for Soviet Jewry, an organization that I helped lead, adamantly opposed violence as a means of social action.

My split with Rabbi Kahane occurred when Iris Kones was killed. Like many Soviet Jewry activists, Rabbi Kahane believed that U.S.-Soviet cultural exchanges should be halted until Soviet Jewry was freed. Rabbi Kahane took this principle to the extreme, however, and in 1972 he inspired a violent attack on the office of Sol Hurok, the impresario who promoted these exchanges. During this attack Hurok's secretary, Iris Kones, was killed. When Rabbi Kahane spoke at my synagogue a few years later, I asked him whether he had supported the action that claimed Kones' life. He said that while he mourned the tragic death of a Jewish woman, he felt it was the price of the Soviet Jewry struggle, much as the Allied bombing of Dresden and Tokyo was part of the price paid for victory in World War II.

I strongly disagreed. There is a great difference between violent attacks as part of state-declared wars and those that are part of self-declared struggles. Individuals have no moral right to make war on their own.

Only once did I stray from this position. In the early 1980s a group of Israeli Jews were involved in four violent incidents; they seriously injured Arab mayors, killed two Arabs in an assault on a PLO university, placed bombs on Arab buses, and plotted to blow up the Temple Mount. While denouncing the last three as random acts of murder or attempted murder, I supported the first, claiming it was a focused reprisal against Arab leaders who had orchestrated the killing of Jews and were calling for more attacks against Jews. At the time, I believed that because the Israeli government was not doing its share to protect the settlers, the settlers had no choice but to protect themselves.

In countless debates, Rabbi Walter Wurzburger pointed out to me that were it not for the mayors incident, the three other underground activities would not have occurred. I have come to understand that Rabbi Wurzburger was right and I was wrong. When judged in a vacuum, perhaps the attacks on the mayors could be defended. However, viewing them in context, I have realized that once individuals assume the right to defend themselves with arms as a means of social action, they open the Pandora's box for other, more random acts of violence. The distance between legitimate and illegitimate acts of violence is a hair's breadth.

The violent underground turned many Israelis against the settlement movement. Historically, violence has a way of doing just that—of disenchanting the populace. The civil rights movement led by Dr. Martin Luther King, Jr., for example, began to wane when violent Black activists came on the scene. Their violence turned many people away from the larger cause.

Of course, rejecting violence often involves difficult choices. During our first protests against the convent at Auschwitz in 1989, my colleagues and I were beaten by Polish workers. Several in our group were itching to fight back, but I strongly counseled against doing so. When I recounted the story in my synagogue upon our return, one congregant rose and said that he had to condemn me in the strongest terms for not hitting back. Jews should never again allow themselves to be beaten at Auschwitz, he proclaimed.

I struggled with this issue for many years. Was I right in demanding that my *chevra* remain passive, or should we have fought back? In retrospect, I still maintain that even though we had been beaten mercilessly, it was precisely our nonviolent reaction that made it possible for our opposition to the convent to be heard around the world.

Nonviolence as a policy has firm roots in our tradition, and specifically in the very text that Rabbi Kahane cited to promote his violent agenda. In explaining why Moses was not allowed to enter the land of Israel, the Midrash records the following conversation between Moses and God. Moses insisted that he deserved immortality. "I'm better than all others," he claimed, pointing out that Adam had disobeyed God by eating from the tree, that Noah had failed to intercede on his doomed generation's behalf, and that Abraham sired an evil son. But God responded, "You killed an Egyptian, the one who was smiting the Jew." "I killed one Egyptian, look how many you have killed!" Moses retorted. "Moses, I give life, and therefore I can take life," God explained.

"You, Moses, are not God. You do not give life, and you therefore cannot take life." For this Midrash, Moses' violent act ought not be applauded. He could have stopped the Egyptian without killing him. So severely was Moses' action regarded, the Midrash suggests, that it was this deed that precluded him from entering the land of Israel.

Torah narrative is complex and ought not to be interpreted simplistically. Far from condoning violence, the narrative of Moses smiting the Egyptian could teach an opposite message that should be etched into the mind and heart of every activist: Violence as a means of social action is immoral and, in the end, counterproductive.

October 1998

Principle Twenty-Four

Understand How to Create a Spiritual Center

Spirituality can be understood as reaching beyond the self to feel the presence of God. The reaching moves in three directions—upward, outward and inward. We strive to reach upward to the Lord above, outward to the "other" in whom the image of God resides, and inward to find our inner goodness, our inner godliness.

One of the most urgent challenges facing American Jews today is how to bring greater spirituality into our synagogues. Spirituality can be understood as reaching beyond the self to feel the presence of God. The reaching moves in three directions-upward, outward, and inward. We strive to reach upward to the Lord above, outward to the "other" in whom the image of God resides, and inward to find our inner goodness, our inner godliness. The three Hebrew terms for synagogue-Beit Midrash, Beit Knesset, and Beit Tefillah-encapsulate the three directions in which spirituality moves and can show us the way to meeting the challenge of bringing greater spirituality to our synagogues.

Beit Midrash, a house of teaching and learning, is where the "upward" values of Torah are taught. The teaching of Torah values, even when those values conflict with contemporary culture, is the first ingredient of spirituality. Within synagogues, spirituality is possible only when there is a readiness to criticize the ethics and materialism of modern society, and, through teaching and learning, offer a higher, Torah-bound alternative.

During much of the twentieth century, Jews who felt themselves to be outsiders in America sought in their synagogues a way to feel that their religion reinforced, indeed, glorified, Americanism and democratic values. Now that we feel at home in America, synagogues have a unique opportunity to restore their spiritual mandate by raising a voice against cultural conformism and seeking a higher distinctiveness that can be a new source of pride.

Some concrete examples: Do our synagogues encourage excess in bar/bat mitzvah or wedding celebrations or do they strive to infuse lifecycle events with higher spiritual meaning? When we distribute honors institutionally, are they based on wealth alone or do they demonstrate our admiration for all who live in accordance with a lofty vision of Jewish values? Is the goal of our sermons and teachings to say what people want to hear, or are we willing to challenge our congregants in order to encourage growth and change? A spiritual synagogue should not only make its congregants comfortable, but also uncomfortable.

Beit Knesset, a house of assembly, is where all come together. Here lies the second "outward" ingredient of spirituality- the readiness to embrace everyone, and especially those in need. The test of spirituality in synagogues is not how the community receives the most powerful, but how it welcomes the most vulnerable. And, are we not, all of us, on some level, vulnerable?

Too many synagogues fail in this mission. The role of a synagogue is to aid and repair the soul, not to pass judgment, condemn, or ostracize. As Rabbi Saul Berman has pointed out, an instructive model for the synagogue is a hospital. Just as a hospital is dedicated to healing physically, so the purpose of the synagogue is to heal spiritually-to bring greater spiritual health. The goal of the synagogue is to admit not only those who are healthy, or to accept only those parts within us that are whole, but also those aspects within each of us that are wounded and in need.

Some suggestions to achieve this goal: Synagogues, including sanctuaries, should be built with ramps to the ark and the lectern.

A beautiful synagogue is one that is accessible, one that sends the message that all are welcome and no one is excluded. Synagogues should also provide resources for the visually and hearing impaired. As for spiritual leaders, rather than sitting apart and in front of the congregation, they should sit among the people, to reinforce the sense of community, the truth that all are of equal importance before God.

Finally, a synagogue is also called a Beit Tefilllah, a house of prayer, of transcendence. Reaching "inward" through prayer, beyond the self, to touch the Divine is the third element of spirituality, and is often by no means easy to accomplish in a synagogue setting. Synagogues are often too caught up in form and structure, in buildings, institutional bureaucracy, shul politics-in the external rather than the internal. But spirituality in synagogues means kindling the spark of God in each of us. Once kindled, our souls can soar to connect to the infinite God and to the godliness in our fellow person.

How? Through song that is participatory and soulful rather than a musical performance in which one is a spectator-song that connects earth and heaven, that binds community, that expresses our deepest emotions and longings. And through dance and reflection. The ritualized words are not meant to exhaust our feelings, but to inspire spontaneous, creative feelings that take us beyond.

Spirituality, moreover, means to begin from wherever we are and never to be complacent, always to aspire to new levels. Spirituality in synagogues is more a process than the achievement of a goal. If we think we've made it, we have failed.

King David asked: "Who will ascend the mountain of the Lord?" The answer is embedded in the question. The one who is constantly seeking is the one who ultimately arrives at the mountain of the Lord. Much like the rebbe who asked his students the following question: "There's a ladder with fifty rungs. One person is on the forty-seventh, the other on the twenty-fifth. Who is higher?" "Of course," his students responded, "the one on the forty-seventh." "No, my children," the rebbe said, "it depends which way you're going." In our synagogues, in our Beit Midrash, our Beit Knesset, and our Beit Tefillah, may we strive always to go in all the right spiritual directions-upward, outward, and inward

September 2000

THE HUMAN FACTOR

The Spiritual Activist keeps in mind the human factors that impact powerfully on the success or failure of a cause, and remembers that as all people are created in the image of God, they have the capacity to make a difference and, with passion, to accomplish the impossible.

The Spiritual Activist learns to cope with fear and to keep laughing even in the direst of circumstances.

The Spiritual Activist remains humble even in high-profile situations, and learns how to deal with the ego and the hubris that access to high places often brings.

The Spiritual Activist remembers to treat others with respect, to be concerned about the personal welfare of those who join the cause, and listen to the voices of those who might disagree.

Principle Twenty-Five

Never Forget the Human Factor

Activists, consumed by a cause, often forget the human factor in their endeavor. This is particularly ironic because the activist is ultimately motivated by concerns for human well-being. A major objective of activism is to struggle against the "I–it" tendency by always keeping in mind activism's "I–thou" essence.

I live in two worlds: the rabbinate and activism. I love the rabbinate. I dread activism.

I once was involved in activism because I enjoyed it, but now I have come to believe that a true activist is one who takes no pleasure from it. Now I'm an activist because I feel I have no choice; there are things I believe I simply must do.

Activism is often impersonal, distant, and harsh. At its foundation is what Martin Buber, the twentieth-century philosopher, would call the "I–it" relationship. In the "I–it" encounter, the "I" relates to the other as an "it," an object devoid of feelings and stripped of godliness. The "I" has no abiding concern with the other in the relationship, because the other is considered just a *thing*. The "I" cares only about the "I"—the self.

The rabbinate, on the other hand, is personal and caring. Buber would characterize the central relationship of the rabbinate as being "I–thou." The "I–thou" encounter is one in which the "I" relates to the other in the relationship as a *subject* full of feeling and pulsating with godliness. This "I" cares about the other in the relationship rather than being self-centered.

Activists, consumed by a cause, often forget the human factor in their endeavor. This is particularly ironic because the activist is ultimately motivated by concern for human well-being. A major objective of activism is to struggle against the "I–it" tendency by always keeping in mind activism's "I–thou" essence.

I started to sense this struggle as I matured as a rabbi. It came to a head in October 1982. I was fasting for a week in front of the Soviet mission to the U.N. in New York in solidarity with Natan Sharansky, then in the midst of a long hunger strike in a Soviet prison. Friends surrounded me and did everything to make my fast easier. When reporters appeared, we would scramble for their attention, not for our own advancement but for the sake of our cause. When the police demanded that we move further away from the mission, we would struggle to stay as close as we could. When KGB agents photographed us from the roof of the mission, some of the protestors would scream, "Russkie, jump!" This cry that emerged from our group was alarming in its reverberations, for it brought home to me that, in our activism, those we were protesting against had become simply The Enemy. We had dehumanized them; they had become the "it."

It was during those turbulent moments of protest that I intensely experienced the darker side of activism. I was caught up in a critical activist struggle but I had sacrificed a key element of my life as a Jew and a rabbi: *menschlichkeit*. Everyone around me had become an "it." Reporters had become objects; they were using us to get a story, and we were using them for publicity. Journalists as well as cops were pawns we were trying to use to promote our cause. The Russian on the roof had become an *ausmensch*; "Let him jump," we had cried.

This event, and the realizations it evoked, became a turning point in my activist life. Since that moment, I have tried to adopt and sustain several guiding principles toward becoming an activist for whom the human element is kept always firmly in sight.

First, I attempt to deal with my opponent humanely in that I refrain from any acts of violence against him, although I do not hesitate to use any other technique of protest that will promote our cause. Second, I recognize that there may be other approaches in combating the wrong that we confront, and I welcome the articulation of these approaches in my synagogue. Third, when the struggle involves a legitimate difference of opinion, such as the varied positions on the current peace process, I seek to understand the other's position; even when that view is antithetical to mine, I attempt to empathize with the conviction that the other feels.

In addition, I try never to forget the human needs of those who are demonstrating alongside me. The safety of my supporters is of paramount concern. And while we must be united at the demonstration itself, I encourage debate and discussion of issues and tactics before we set out. Activism, when it is authentic, should have a human face.

This point was affirmed for me in a very powerful way just two weeks ago on the Saturday night of our demonstration in Oslo protesting the Arafat Nobel peace prize. We gathered with the families of the victims of Arafat's terrorism, holding up placards. Potentially this could have been another typical "I–it" situation: police mounted on horses; attack dogs off to the side; TV cameras everywhere as we jockeyed for position to be seen; slogans shouted out at those entering the Oslo city hall to attend the ceremony.

Toward the end, out of the corner of my eye, I noticed a young boy, about six years old, desperately holding on to his mother's hand. There was a look of terror on his face. I walked toward him and lifted him. "Why are you here?" I asked. He could not answer. Tears welled from his eyes. The boy's mother explained: "This is my son. His father was the bus driver murdered in the Afula attack." I embraced the child for several moments. After demonstrating for hours, the "thou" element had asserted itself in the activist arena.

It is always a struggle to fuse *menschlichkeit* with activism. But if one does not try, the activism is hollow.

January 1995

Principle Twenty-Six

Everyone Can Make a Difference

While no one is indispensable, no one is dispensable either. Moreover, not only is the human being unique, but every action can be similarly viewed as having unique power. Maimonides makes this point when he declares that one should look at the world as an evenly balanced scale. The next action we undertake or don't undertake has the potential to tip the scale one way or the other.

Dr. Harry Emerson Fosdick, the noted preacher, tells of a conversation between an astronomer and a philosopher. The astronomer asks, "Astronomically speaking, what is man?" The philosopher responds, "Astronomically speaking, man is the astronomer."

Both arguments, writes Rabbi Joseph Lookstein, are provocative and challenging. If we consider the speed of light, the vastness of the universe, and the distance between planets, human beings are reduced to but a speck in the larger whole. Yet Fosdick's philosopher manages to restore the human being to a level of significance by pointing out that it is only because of the genius of the human mind, with its unique ability to compute and calculate and its curiosity about the nature of the universe, that the astronomer's question has any meaning at all.

Certainly, the realization of each individual's relative insignificance in the larger scheme of things is an existential issue with which every person must grapple. What, for example, can we

Jewish activists possibly hope to accomplish with our protests? Why even bother to confront the Soviets on Soviet Jewry, the Syrians on the Israeli MIAs, or the Argentinians on the welfare of the Argentine Jewish community? After all, these governments are so large and powerful and we are so small. What impact can we possibly have?

Addressing this issue, the Talmud in *Sanhedrin* first points out that since all of the people who today compose humankind originated from the same source—Adam—none of us can claim to be better than anyone else. This teaching promulgates the idea of the commonality of all people—that is, no human being is of special significance.

The Talmud then teaches an opposite lesson. Just as in the beginning of time the world started with one person, Adam, upon whom the entire world depended—had Adam been destroyed, all would have been destroyed—so too we, as Adam's descendants, are equally important. In the words of the Talmud: "If a person prints many coins from one die, each one is a replica of the other, but the Holy One Blessed Be He stamped every person with the die of Adam and yet no one exactly resembles his fellow." In other words, Adam was unique. There was no other beside him. Today there are billions of us but each individual is similarly unique. In short, while no one is indispensable, no one is dispensable either.

Maimonides takes this idea a step further. Not only is the human being unique, but every action can be similarly viewed as having unique power. Maimonides makes this point when he declares that one should look at the world as an evenly balanced scale. The next action we undertake or don't undertake has the potential to tip the scale one way or the other.

Nehama Leibowitz, the late great biblical scholar, embellishes on Maimonides's point: "Just as each individual is endowed with his own unique personality and has no exact counterpart, so every deed committed in the world makes its own particular contribution, positive or negative, to the general welfare, ultimately affecting the fate of the whole of mankind . . . every act, however minute, is fraught with consequences for the future, as far as his environment and beyond are concerned."

It is here that the rationalist and kabbalist part company. For the rationalist, not every action has impact. Still, the sage Ben Azzai says, "Do not be scornful of any person and do not be disdainful of any thing, for you have no person without his hour, and no thing without its place." As Andy Warhol put it, every person will have his fifteen minutes of fame.

The kabbalists see it differently. For them, every action, even those that appear irrelevant, has impact. Everything we do affects everything in our environment, which in turn affects other environments—in the end changing the entire world.

A key refrain of activists is a comment often made by Rav Shlomo Carlebach: "You never know." For Maimonides, you never know which action will resonate immediately or in the future, in a kind of delayed reaction. In other words, every action has the potential to precipitate change. The kabbalists would add that this is true even if the change is not discernible.

Just as every person and every action can precipitate change, so too can impact be made in small increments even when one is unable to realize total victory. A story illustrates this point.

An elderly sage sat on a beach, casting starfish back into the ocean. "What are you doing?" inquired a youngster. "A high tide washed thousands of these fish ashore. I'm throwing them back into the water before they bake in the sun." "Foolish man," the youngster retorted, "thousands of fish are around you. Your efforts are futile, you'll make no difference." Picking up one fish, the elderly man threw it back into the sea. Looking at the youngster, he said, "Well, for this fish it makes all the difference."

The spiritual activist needs to keep in his or her consciousness the wisdom of that long ago sage so as to avoid becoming discouraged or feeling that there is little one can accomplish in the face of the overwhelming amount of injustice, violence, hunger and pain that exist in the world. Of course, none of us alone can end evil and oppression in the world, abolish hunger and poverty or end human suffering. None of us alone can ensure the safety of Israel or the survival of the Jewish people.

Yet, each of us *can* make all the difference for another individual. Each of us *can* succor someone in pain or hunger. Each of us *can* help win justice for someone unfairly accused. Indeed, each of us is capable of saving another person or more than one person. Working together, we can save many people and do our part to ensure a future for the Jewish people as a whole and for all of humankind. All of us, with the help of God, can make a difference.

December 1996

Principle Twenty-Seven

With Passion the Impossible
Can Be Accomplished

The principle that, with passion the impossible can be accomplished, is built into one of the most important concepts in Judaism—every human being is created in the image of God. As God is infinite, so too do we created in God's image, have the power to be godly, to reach beyond our grasp, to do that which we never believed we could do. The very term spiritual activism denotes how the spirit of God can work through people.

Anatoly Sharansky is more than merely a person. Arrested five years ago by the Soviet regime, he was sentenced to a thirteen-year prison term on charges that he worked for the Central Intelligence Agency, an allegation denied by President Jimmy Carter. Before his arrest, he was an active member of the Helsinki Watch Committee, and he agitated for the right of Jews to emigrate to Israel. Thus he is being oppressed not only as a man, but also as a representative of the human spirit, and particularly of the Jewish quest to be identified with the people and land of Israel.

Those of us who have never met him have come to know him through his wife, Avital. On the morning after their wedding eight years ago, Avital, who had received permission to emigrate, left the Soviet Union with the assurance that her husband would join her within six months. She was further informed that if she did not leave then, she would find it virtually impossible to leave later. As time passed, it became clear that the Kremlin had no intention of granting Anatoly a visa. During their separation, Avital has labored tirelessly to bring his plight before the world. If you have not seen her pain, you cannot understand the meaning of anguish. Recently Anatoly embarked on a hunger strike to protest the cutting off of the very few letters and visits that he had been permitted yearly.

Many people have tried to reach out to the Sharanskys, to tell them that others really care. I too have tried. For six consecutive days, beginning October 31, I fasted in front of the Soviet Mission to the United Nations. During this period, I was joined by well over one thousand people who, on a daily basis, fasted, prayed, studied the Bible, and protested on Avital's' behalf. I did not embark on this enterprise merely to test myself or to discover what it would be like. For this form of protest to have an impact on those who are holding Anatoly, it was necessary that the public hear about it.

The block where the Soviet Mission is situated, 67th Street between Third and Lexington Avenues, is oppressive. Sitting behind police barriers, diagonally across from the Soviet Mission, we felt imprisoned. K.G.B. spies peered from the roof; FBI agents took photographs from the ground level; the police often made life miserable for the demonstrators; and the irate tenants, annoyed by our presence, dropped water and eggs from apartment windows. Although we had voluntarily imprisoned ourselves in an open street, we could get up and walk away whenever we chose; Anatoly cannot.

A hunger strike is exhilarating but painful. At night you feel hunger pangs; during the day you feel weak, your legs wobble, you're ready to keel over. To fast, you must be totally committed to the cause, and the mind must overcome the body's needs. When you are alone, the body predominates and hunger seems intolerable; when surrounded by friends, you feel reinforced and find it possible to continue. Fasting among supporters is not real fasting; but Anatoly in the gulag, alone—that's a true hunger strike.

On the fourth day, Avital joined us. Her eyes reflected her sadness. When asked to say a few words, she responded: "I can't speak now. All I can do is cry." A friend explained, "The joy Avital feels in seeing people who empathize with her and Anatoly has moved her to speak without words, to speak with tears." When Avital was leaving, she said: "We are one. We are together." But the truth was that in the end, we would go back to our families while she would remain alone.

By the fifth day a "high" had set in—one not imposed from the outside but generated from within. When one is fasting, the energy normally used to consume and digest food is deflected elsewhere. Intellectual and spiritual powers seem to be expanded rather than diminished. Inner masks are removed. No food clogs the body. One becomes more honest, more open, more expressive of one's feelings.

Russian diplomats came and went in droves, looking harried, ambivalent about what was happening. I knew the Russians were people, but I wondered whether they could really display emotion. Can they laugh, cry, love? As the new leader, Yuri V. Adropov assumes power, will he make a gesture of good faith by freeing Anatoly?

Will the political leaders of our country, when speaking with Mr. Andropov, mention Anatoly by name? Or will the discussion focus only on such issues as Poland and Afghanistan—masses, not individuals; countries, not people?

As I look back at that week, it seems unreal. I never imagined I could endure such a long hunger strike. I came to realize that when motivated, there is little one, with the help of God, cannot do. And so, Anatoly found the strength to fast for a hundred and ten days—and, I, in a small gesture of support, did so for six days.

The principle that with passion the impossible can be accomplished, is built into one of the most important concepts in Judaism—every human being is created in the image of God. As God is infinite, so too do we, created in God's image, have the power to be godly, to reach beyond our grasp, to do that which we never believed we could do. The very term spiritual activism denotes how God can work through people.

Such was the power of that Sabbath to Sabbath fast. It transcended time and space. It's as if those days didn't exist—an empty space in my life. For Anatoly such emptiness has continued for years. But in emptiness there is often deep meaning. The Sharanskys, in fighting for human rights, lead full lives.

December 1982

Principle Twenty-Eight

Learn to Cope with Fear

What do we do when we're afraid? Do we become immobilized, unable go forward, or do we gather strength in an attempt to meet the challenges that lie ahead? Feelings may be involuntary, but actions can be controlled. Alternatively, the higher fear of God removes the lesser fears that invariably affect every human being.

After spending a Shabbat in Bergen-Belsen to protest President Reagan's visit there in May 1985, our group was asked by the head of the Jewish community there to leave. "Your stay will jeopardize the safety of German Jewry," we were told.

In November of that year, during the first Reagan–Gorbachev summit in Geneva, representatives of the local Jewish community declined to sing "Hatikvah" after a rally for Soviet Jews. "This is Switzerland. We don't want to jeopardize our stay here," they told us.

In July 1986, when we were in Vienna to demonstrate against the inauguration of Kurt Waldheim, who had been elected president of Austria, Jewish shop owners implored us to go. "They'll break the windows of our stores," they said, recalling the horror of Kristallnacht, November 1938, the "Night of Broken Glass."

A common theme emerged from all these communities: Jews were afraid.

These incidents raise some important questions: Is fear a positive emotion? Does fear suggest a lack of faith? How does one cope with fear?

One Jewish scholar who struggled with these questions was Isaac Abrabanel who lived in Spain in the latter part of the fifteenth century. Abrabanel suggests that fear is not a sign of either cowardice or weakness. It is simply part of the human condition, a feeling that, like all feelings, is neither right nor wrong; it just is.

The person who is afraid should not be judged harshly; nor should that person judge him or herself harshly when overcome by fear. For who among us has never been afraid?

Even Israeli generals, when they look deep inside themselves, admit to feeling fear. Once after being introduced as a "fearless soldier," General Ariel Sharon scrupulously took pains to disavow the description. "When I crossed the Suez Canal in the '73 war," he said, "I was frightened. Only a fool doesn't fear, but we went forward."

There is no one who is not afraid at one time or another. The real question is. "What do we do when we're afraid?" Do we become immobilized, unable to go forward, or do we gather strength in an attempt to meet the challenges that lie ahead? Feelings may be involuntary, but actions can be controlled.

Abrabanel, who was involved in the political world of Spain, instinctively felt that fear could not be overcome; it could only be dealt with through action. As a man of action, he understood the inevitability of fear, and its only antidote—action.

Rav Yosef Dov Soloveitchik approaches the issue differently. Everyone, suggests Rav Soloveitchik, seems beset with fears of some kind. Some are afraid they will not succeed in their careers, others fear losing wealth or status, and still others are afraid of sickness, physical weakness, or poverty. But such fears may be utterly wiped out by a greater fear. That fear is the fear of the Lord. From his prison cell in Chistopol, Natan Sharansky wrote that an idea from the book of Proverbs helped him defy the KGB: "The beginning of wisdom is to fear the Lord."

For Rav Soloveitchik, Modern Orthodoxy's most eminent Talmudist and philosopher, the higher fear of God removes the lesser fears that invariably affect every human being. From this perspective even the fear of God does not denote a stern attribute of the Almighty. It is rather an expression of God's love of all people. After all, by fearing God, we're able to quash other fundamental human fears. But even for Rav Soloveitchik, fear can never be completely overcome, as one's belief in God is never perfect. Even the greatest of believers may have some infinitesimal doubt. Therefore some elements of fundamental fear remains.

Despite the teachings of Abrabanel and despite Rav Soloveitchik's philosophy of coping with fear, Jews remain afraid, not only European Jews but American Jews as well.

Many American Jews are afraid to speak out for Jonathan Pollard, fearful of charges of dual loyalty. In fact, the Pollard case has nothing to do with dual loyalty; the excessiveness of the sentence is a perversion of American justice.

Likewise, many Jews warned us not to sue Poland's Cardinal Glemp for slander after his outrageous claims that we came to murder nuns and destroy the convent at Auschwitz. In their words, "There are a billion Catholics out there." In fact, if we've learned anything from the Shoah, it is that if we cave in to an anti-Semite, we inspire greater anti-Semitism.

Also during the Crown Heights pogrom and for months later, too many Jews distanced themselves from expressing solidarity with their brothers and sisters there. During that time, Jews should have run *to* Crown Heights rather than *from* Crown Heights.

A telling example of the fear of American Jews was the reaction to the visit of Nelson Mandela to New York in June 1990. He was feted with a ticker-tape parade down Broadway with Jewish leadership prominently in the forefront. At the time, I wondered, had Natan Sharansky, despite his record as a champion of human rights, been pro-apartheid, which of course he's not, would he have been received as a hero in New York? Certainly not. Then why should Mandela, who is indeed a champion of the anti-apartheid struggle, be accorded such a welcome, having embraced such tyrants as Muammar Khaddafi, Fidel Castro, and Yasir Arafat. In the end, a few of us stood alone protesting the parade. Our message was clear: If you embrace Arafat, you bring shame to the anti-apartheid struggle.

Several days later on ABC-TV's *Nightline*, Mandela praised Castro. He then flew to Miami, where he was greeted by thousands of protesting Cuban Americans. The actions of the Cuban Americans, when contrasted with those of American Jews, raise the question: Why did Cuban Americans demonstrate against Mandela for his praise of Castro, while American Jews did not protest his embrace of Arafat, whose hands are dripping with Jewish blood? Clearly Cuban Americans are not afraid. American Jews are. Why is this so? The answer seems to be that Cuban Americans are willing to stand firm on their principles while American Jews, especially those in leadership, who are blessed with much, deep down are afraid that by speaking out they will become vulnerable. The reverse is true. The more one speaks out for a beleaguered community, the more that community is protected rather than rendered vulnerable.

When in Rome in June 1987 to protest the Vatican's embrace of Austria's president Kurt Waldheim, an unrepentant Nazi, I witnessed a vivid example of a greater fear subduing a lesser, a deliberate action overcoming uncontrollable fear. When our group first arrived in Rome, the local Jewish community was paralyzed with fear and refused to participate in our demonstration. By the end of our visit, however, five hundred Roman Jews marched with us to the Vatican. As we stood in Vatican Square, I spoke to the group about Titus, who, after the destruction of the Second Temple, marched the Jews down the Tiber River as slaves to build the Coliseum. Today we marched as free Jews. We were not groveling; we stood strong.

What inspired these young women and men to calm their fears and join us? It could have been the greater fear of God. Or perhaps it was pride in the state of Israel that motivated them to act in a conscious fashion to allay their fears. Or maybe it was simply the reassuring sense that they were part of a larger community. Who knows?

As we stood in Vatican Square, the group began to sing the words of Rabbi Nahman of Bratslav: "The whole world is a very narrow bridge, but the main thing is not to be afraid at all." In so far as fear can be subdued, Rav Nahman's motto is one that German, Swiss, Austrian, and yes, American Jews should remember well.

August 1993

Principle Twenty-Nine

Know How to Laugh

For activists, laughter may be of particular importance. It's a reminder not to take oneself too seriously, especially in uneven situations involving direct confrontation with power. Laughter in such settings teaches humility, restores one's sense of proportion. Laughter must accompany us as we protest, as we cry out. It's our way of declaring that in the end, against all odds, *Am Yisrael chai* — we will prevail.

Natan Sharansky had just been released from the Gulag. His last steps to freedom across the Glienicke Bridge connecting East and West Germany were seen around the world. Having reached the end of his almost nine-year ordeal in Soviet labor camps, he was well aware that there had been a worldwide campaign in his behalf. What was he thinking about as he strode across that bridge? His years in prison? The future? Thoughts about thanksgiving and gratitude to God?

When weeks later I asked him that question, Natan responded that what he was thinking about was the pair of pants the Soviets had given him upon his release. The pants were too large. As he took that famous walk to freedom, the overriding thought in his head was this: Oh God, please don't let my pants fall down!

With all that he had endured, Sharansky was blessed with the ability to see the lighter side even in his darkest hours. And, after his release he didn't forget the power of laughter. Take, for example, the day he was returning to Israel after one of his early visits to the United States. Standing in the Kennedy Airport terminal, a short man, even shorter than Sharansky—approached. Placing his black yarmulke on Natan's head, he said in a deep Yiddish, *"Gib mir a berachah."* Natan seemed confused. And so, I turned to him and said, "Natan, you're not going to believe this, but you've become a chassidishe rebbe. This man wants a blessing from you." "You don't understand," Natan told the man, "I'm not a rebbe, he (pointing to me) is a rabbi. He'll bless you." "No," the man firmly replied. "I know who he is, and I have no interest in his blessing—only yours. And," he added lovingly, "Mr. Sharansky, I will not move from here until you give me a *berachah.*" "Natan," I said, "you may have overcome the K.G.B., but this R'Yid you're not going to beat. You've got a plane to catch. Just put your hands on his head and give him a *berachah* and let's go." With a twinkle in his eye, Natan placed his hands on the gentleman's head and said, *"Baruch Atah Hashem, Elokeinu Melech Ha-olam, ha-motzi lechem min ha-aretz"* (the blessing recited before eating bread). It was Natan's way of laughing at himself and declaring his unworthiness to give a blessing. What struck me as even more humorous was the man's reaction. Taking back his yarlmulke, he walked off ecstatic, absolutely delighted. Natan may have believed his blessing was worth nothing; this man thought it was worth everything.

Of course, Natan's ability to laugh, to see the lighter side, did not prevent him from appreciating the seriousness of the course he had taken, nor did it prevent him from reflecting deeply on his mission or feeling justifiably enraged at how grievously he had been mistreated. His defiant courage in standing up to the Soviets was one of the finest hours of Jewish heroism in our century. Still, he never forgot how to see the humor in a situation.

For activists, laughter may be of particular importance. First of all it's a reminder not to take oneself too seriously, especially in uneven situations involving direct confrontation with power. Laughter in such settings teaches humility, restores one's sense of proportion.

An example of this laughter occurred in July of 1989, when after
many weeks of planning we jumped the fence at Auschwitz.
Standing before the cameras of the world I called out, "We've come
to demand that the covenant be moved." Jacob Davidson, a young
heroic man, mature beyond his years, nudged me—"Avi," he whis-
pered, "that's the wrong demonstration. It's the convent, not the
covenant [of the P.L.O.]." There we were, all seven of us confronting the Vatican and the whole Roman Catholic church. And,
as if that were not funny enough, I call the convent the covenant.

Rabbi Nahman of Bratslav, the great Chassidic master, taught
another lesson about laughter that the activist ought to remember.
"There is no peace in the world, because there is too much anger.
You can only make peace with joy." These words seem to speak
almost directly to the activist. Rare is the activist who is not to some
degree angry. What the activist can learn from Rabbi Nahman's
words here is that joy—in this case laughter—can ameliorate the
anger and hasten the peace. The activist whose larger goal is to fix
the world laughs. Laughter is the pathway to redemption.

Rav Shlomo Carlebach approached laughter differently. For
him, laughter meant accepting whatever God doles out. Once, Rav
Shlomo offered his coat as a warm "bed" for a stray cat he had
found in his hotel lobby. The cat soiled the coat and the house-
keeping staff threw it out. Told he had lost his coat, Rav Shlomo
laughed. Never mind that in its pockets were his money, his pass-
port, his plane tickets, his schedule. Still he laughed, accepting
what God had given him. We activists would do well to learn from
Rav Shlomo: Do our best, laugh, and accept whatever happens for
the good.

Interestingly, the Hebrew word *litzchok*, "to laugh," is similar
to the word *litzok*, which can be translated as "to cry." In the
Hebrew language the guttural letters *chet* and *ayyin* often inter-
change, rendering *litzchok* and *litzok* the same, thus illustrating the
fundamental connection between laughter and tears.

Sometimes when one looks at a child, it is difficult to know
whether the child is laughing or crying. On many occasions I have

sat with people in grief and been struck by the quick mood changes. Often it was difficult to discern whether what I was witnessing were tears of laughter or of sorrow.

Perhaps the association in the Hebrew language between the words for laughing and for crying can also teach a lesson about conquering despair. No matter how bleak the situation, no matter how dark the circumstances, no matter how profound the tears, laughter is not far away. One should never give up.

The second of our three patriarchs is called Yitzchak (Isaac), which literally means "will laugh." He was given this name because his parents, Sarah and Abraham, laughed when told that at their advanced age a child would be born to them. The commentators ask why he was called *Yitzchak*—"to laugh" in the future tense. He should have been called *Tzachak*, "he laughed." It can be suggested that Yitzchak is in the future tense because it refers not only to him but to the totality of Jewish history. Just as Yitzchak was born against all odds and through his birth the covenant with Abraham and Sarah continued, so would his descendants face innumerable challenges, would time and again be counted out, but in the end would prevail.

A classic talmudic story echoes this idea. After the destruction of the Second Temple, Rabbi Akiva and his colleagues were walking near the Temple Mount and saw a fox roaming among its ruins. Akiva laughed even as his colleagues began to weep. "Why are you laughing?" his colleagues asked. "Why are you crying?" Akiva retorted. "The Temple is now in ruins," they said. Akiva responded: "Until the prophecy that the Temple would be destroyed came true, I was unsure whether the prophecy of rebuilding would be fulfilled. Now that the Temple has been decimated, rebirth is certain." Akiva's colleagues turned to him and said, "You have comforted us, Akiva, you have comforted us."

Such is the power of laughter. It must accompany us as we protest, as we cry out. It's our way of declaring that in the end, against all odds, *Am Yisrael chai*—we will prevail.

June 1997

Principle Thirty

Leadership Sometimes Requires Quiet Strength

There are different models of leadership. One is the "rah-rah" type of leader who raises a voice loudly and insistently on behalf of a cause. The other is the activist whose strength is transmitted through a calmness that speaks louder than words.

At times I'm asked to name the greatest activist I ever knew. Without hesitation I have always given the same response—Avital Sharansky. Avital is the person who, in my view, represents the activist par excellence of the latter half of the twentieth century. Avital is, of course, the wife of Natan Sharansky, the most famous former Soviet Jewish Prisoner of Zion, and, today, Israel's Interior Minister.

To understand Avital's greatness, it is crucial to recognize that there are different models of leadership. One is the "rah-rah" type of leader who raises a voice loudly and insistently on behalf of a cause. The other is the activist whose strength is transmitted through a calmness that speaks louder than words.

The narrative in the Torah that most reflects why the second model of leadership is the superior one is a story from the life of Elijah the Prophet found in the Book of Kings. Upset that the people of Israel were turning away from God, Elijah flees to the wilderness. "What are you doing here?" asks God. Elijah replies, "I have been zealous for the Lord...the children of Israel have forsaken Your covenant...and I alone remain."

Then, in rapid succession, the prophet witnesses a wild storm, hears a loud noise, and, lastly, sees a fire spring up out of nowhere. After these manifestations, Elijah is told that God can neither be seen nor heard in any of the above. Finally, a small, still voice is heard—a *"kol demamah dakah"*—teaching that it is in this small, still voice that God can be found.

Not fully comprehending the point God is trying to convey, Elijah again declares, "I am zealous for You, oh God." The Lord then instructs him to appoint Elisha as his successor. Because Elijah had failed to understand the power of the soft and modest voice, he is no longer deemed suitable to lead his people.

Rabbi David Silber notes that Elijah failed to learn from the revelation of the Torah at Sinai. While the first Ten Declarations (commonly translated Ten Commandments) were given by God to Moses with much thunder and lightning, in the end, they lay shattered on the ground. The second time, however, the Declarations were given more modestly, without such fanfare. And they remain. We are, in no small measure, the people of the second Ten Declarations. They are the ones that have endured. This teaches us that the most powerful voice is not necessarily the loudest one. Rather, it is often the soft voice which permeates the soul and inspires people to change their lives.

Avital was that kind of strong but quiet leader. In my years of traveling with her around North America, drumming up support on behalf of Natan, I came to know how Avital conducted herself in this manner. There is the image of Avital quietly approaching President Reagan at the White House on Human Rights Day to ask him in a soft and humble voice to extend himself to save Natan from the Soviet gulag. There is the image of Avital beseeching Jewish Federation leaders in a Washington hotel not to forget her husband, and then announcing almost as an afterthought that she would be walking to the Soviet Embassy immediately thereafter. She did so, and moved by her quiet eloquence, hundreds of her listeners spontaneously followed her out the door. There is the image of Avital stepping off a plane in San Antonio to a greeting from a throng of school children waving Israeli flags. Children, the epitome of innocence, responded enthusiastically to Avital's quiet strength.

Whenever I reflect on Avital and her long, arduous, and, finally, successful campaign to win the release of Natan, I remember that wherever we went, she would always listen intently to the views of the people with whom we met. Avital was always ready to step aside and give others a sense of ownership, a sense that they were playing critical roles in securing Natan's release. To this day, many people believe that it was through their efforts that Natan was freed.

This, I believe, is the sign of true leadership. Rather than grabbing the spotlight, Avital always stepped back. Nevertheless, despite this self-effacing quality, or perhaps because of it, light seemed to shine even more powerfully upon her.

To be sure, there are times when one must speak from a position of power and Avital knew how to do that as well. Yet, in the end, her real strength, which set her apart from so many others, was that she understood that the message of God that resonates the most powerfully is the one heard in the still small voice. It is only when we are in concert with that voice that we can change the destiny of the Jewish people and the world.

Most people die with their mouths open. Perhaps this is meant to serve as an ironic reminder that in life it is sometimes more important to listen than to speak. And when we do speak, we should remember the power of speaking softly, thereby prompting others to lean toward us in order to hear our message better and then to follow through all the more faithfully.

July 1999

Principle Thirty-One

Tame the Ego

Understanding that the world was created for each of us individually empowers us to believe that we each have the potential to change the world in our separate and unique ways. Yet the danger certainly exists that if the ego of an activist is not kept tightly in check, it can eventually overwhelm or subtly subvert the endeavor to which that activist is dedicated.

A story is told of a Chassidic rabbi who carried two notes in his pocket. One stated, "The world was created for me." The second declared, "I am like dust of the earth."

As with life itself, the key to being a successful activist lies in maintaining a healthy balance between these two concepts. If we tip too far in either direction, we will not be able to realize our full potential as activists or make our fullest contribution to the causes about which we care most passionately.

Understanding that the world was created for us individually empowers us to believe that we each have the potential to change the world in our separate and unique ways. Without this core belief, there is little that an activist will be able to accomplish.

The Midrash argues that having a healthy ego is not necessarily a negative for a person. Commenting on the verse, "And you shall love the Lord your God with all your heart," the rabbis note that the Hebrew for heart (*lev*) is written in the plural (*levavchah*). Since the heart symbolizes human nature, the use of the plural here is viewed by the rabbis as meaning that God is to be worshiped with both the good and bad inclinations. Paradoxically, our need for ego gratification can be a factor in spurring us to undertake beneficial efforts on behalf of people in need.

Yet the danger certainly exists that if the ego of an activist is not kept tightly in check, it can eventually overwhelm or subtly subvert the endeavor to which that activist is dedicated. All too often, the strategy best suited for promoting an activist leader personally conflicts with the strategy most likely to bring success to the larger cause. Additionally, an egotistical leader may come to justify expending time, money, and energy that are crucial to the long-term success of the struggle on the more enticing short-term goal of personal advancement. Finally, if people come to perceive that a particular activist leader is simply a self-promoter, that understanding will raise questions in the public mind as to the legitimacy of the cause to which that leader is dedicated.

Given the importance of keeping the ego in check, how can this be accomplished? One pathway is to learn the trait of humility; after all, humility is the antedote to being caught up in the self, in the ego.

Maimonides argues that in life one should always strive for and practice moderation. There is a notable exception to this approach in his teachings; he insists that a good man or woman must evince humility at all times. Why does the great sage make this exception? He explains that since it is a natural tendency for every human being to seek honor, only by counterbalancing that drive with extreme humility will one truly be able to walk the "middle road."

Another pathway to living humbly is found in the biblical story of Moses. Moses is described as the humblest of people. Hence, when Moses is told that two men were prophesying in the camp he declares, "if only all the Lord's people were prophets." Feeling unworthy, Moses concludes that if he can prophesy so can others.

But a closer look may suggest an opposite idea. Moses' gracious act may have reflected his self confidence rather than his meekness. Assured of his own capabilities he was not threatened by others who were prophesying. Indeed, humility doesn't mean thinking little of oneself. All of us created in the image of God should feel a sense of self worth in our abilities to succeed. It is this confidence that gave Moses the inner strength to share leadership with others.

From this perspective, humility is the assessing of oneself in relationship to God. It is within that comparison that one recognizes how small one is. In fact, the closer one is to God, and Moses was the closest to Him, the more one recognizes one's finitude in comparison to God's infinite nature.

An important lesson emerges from the Moses story. Too often leaders are reluctant to surround themselves with the highest-quality people out of fear that these assistants or advisors may eventually supplant them in the top position. A first-rate leader, on the other hand, comes to understand with humility the message of limitation. It is simply impossible to do it all by oneself. One test of a quality leader, whether in the activist world or in other realms, is whether he or she is secure enough to bring in the most competent associates, and then to give them the opportunity to make decisions on their own. In the end, accepting such indispensable help will further the cause for which the leader is fighting, even if it has the effect of slightly diffusing his or her own personal power.

In my own life as an activist, the struggle to free Jonathan Pollard from prison illustrates this tension between the self and the cause. After serving as Jonathan's personal rabbi for eight years, Jonathan cut off contact with me charging bitterly that I had not been responsive enough to his needs. It was a painful blow, one that made me face some serious soul-searching. Should I give in to my own deeply felt sense of personal hurt and separate myself from Jonathan and his cause, or should I continue to advocate publicly on behalf of his freedom? From this rupture I came to understand even more clearly that one's personal feelings had to be subordinated to the larger cause. Ultimately, a cause worth fighting for is bigger than any and all of its adherents.

I remember vividly the moment Natan Sharansky stepped off the plane in Israel. Thousands had gathered to hear the words of the great hero of our people, who had survived nine bitter years in Soviet prison camps. On the dais were people jockeying for position to get close enough to Natan so that they would show up on television or in the morning papers alongside him. Yet standing unobtrusively in the back of the crowd and making no attempt to elbow himself into position alongside Natan was Rabbi Zvi Tau, who had served for years as Avital's (Natan's wife) personal rabbi. In reality, Rabbi Tau was in many ways the central most important figure, other than Avital and other members of Natan's family, in the international campaign to win Natan's release. Still, as leaders pressed themselves forward into the limelight, Rabbi Tau stood quietly and modestly in the back row. Sometimes the most important people are not those in the spotlight, but rather those who stand humbly in the background.

Rabbi Tau had enough self-confidence in his own ability to change the world that he was able to mastermind and implement much of the plan to free Natan and to keep believing in it through the bleak periods when even other staunch supporters all but despaired of the hope that Sharansky would ever emerge alive from the gulag. Yet this remarkable individual also had the maturity and insight to understand that success is not ultimately measured in photo opportunities, sound bites, or frequent mentions in the *New York Times*. Rabbi Tau understood the message of the two notes of that Chassidic rabbi.

June 1998

Principle Thirty-Two

Don't Be Seduced by Access to Power

It is too often the case that those who speak to the president temper their views, soften their language. Their primary goal is to ensure continued access. But integral to access is the burden of responsibility that must accompany it. A basic principle of activism is that access should never lead to a compromise in integrity.

The day after President Bill Clinton rejected the request to commute Jonathan Pollard's sentence to time served, he met with leaders of the Conference of Presidents of Major American Jewish Organizations. No one present mentioned Jonathan's name. The president, no doubt, assumed that the Jewish community concurred with his decision—or at the very least was not too deeply troubled by it. Otherwise someone would surely have raised a voice of protest.

One of the likely reasons that Jonathan's commutation has been denied is that since his incarceration ten years ago his case has never been on the formal agenda of a meeting between any U.S. president and Jewish organization leaders. We cannot expect the president of the United States to do what we do not demand of him.

It is too often the case that those who speak to people in positions of power temper their views, soften their language. Their primary goal is to ensure continued access. But integral to access is the burden of responsibility that must accompany it. A basic prin-

ciple of activism is that access should never lead to a compromise
in integrity.

I know firsthand the enormous challenges and dangers that
the principle of "access responsibility" poses. After the bombing in
Buenos Aires a year ago (July 1994), I traveled to Argentina to give
comfort to the injured and families of victims. A friend arranged
for me to meet Argentine president Carlos Menem. As the private
hour-long meeting closed, Menem told me that in order to elabo-
rate for me his efforts to apprehend the terrorists, he would convene an extraordinary cabinet session that afternoon, carefully
scheduled to allow me to return to my hosts prior to Shabbat.

As I sat at Menem's side during the cabinet meeting, I felt
myself in danger of being seduced by the access I had received. I
had to remind myself over and over that the honor I had been
accorded should not deter me from protesting if I determined that
Menem was insincere.

Soon after, convinced that the Menem government was in fact
not doing enough to tighten security and apprehend the suspects,
I strongly protested when Menem was given the Statesman of the
Year Award by the Appeal for Conscience Foundation the following October in New York. I was told afterward that Menem was
incensed. "I give this man honor," he declared, "and this is what
he does!"

But the event that will forever be etched in my mind as illustrative of how access can blind the best of people occurred in May
1978. President Carter was pushing through Congress the sale of
F-15 planes to Saudi Arabia. Jews in America were incensed.

In a brilliant tactical move, Carter invited more than a thousand Jewish leaders to the White House for a hastily organized celebration of Israel's thirtieth anniversary, together with then Israeli
prime minister Menachem Begin. With just a few days prepara-
tion, the event was successfully pulled off. Many of the same
Jewish leaders who had refused to join in a massive anti-Carter
protest that was being planned at the White House decided to
attend. And, horror of horrors, rather than voicing protest, they

were all on their best behavior. In fact, on that very day, Carter announced the U.S. government's intent to establish a U.S. Holocaust Museum. All of this was a transparent attempt to appease the Jewish community with glitz, *kavod* (honor), and the Holocaust to boot.

I too decided to attend, in the hope that I would find an opportunity to protest directly to the president. I joined the throng that lined up to shake his hand. As I waited my turn, I began to feel the pomp and grandeur of the White House and wondered whether I could speak truth to power. Memorizing the words I wanted to say to the president, in fear that I would freeze when meeting him, I finally clasped his hand and said, "I was one of your strongest supporters, but I'm outraged by your disastrous tilt toward the Arabs. And Mr. President, don't give us the Holocaust at the expense of Israel." The president looked incensed, but I felt good that access had not prompted me to compromise my principles.

For years I have noticed in the offices of rabbis and Jewish leaders photos of them shaking hands with Mr. Carter that day— pictures that the White House sent to every attendee together with a letter of personal greetings from the president. Rather than feeling duped, most participants viewed that day as glorious; they display it for all to see, much like a badge of honor. Such is the allure of access.

There is one other access principle that must be underscored. Those who have constant access should recognize that government leaders do not necessarily always take them seriously. Politicians know that those with access are often the ones who compromise on speaking the truth. The truth is that those who are on the inside often don't say it the way it is. Those who are on the outside, at the gates, are often able to speak more powerfully and honestly.

Present at the meeting the day after President Clinton denied Pollard commutation was one of Pollard's supporters. He was later asked why he did not raise the Pollard issue, thereby leaving the impression that business was to be conducted as usual even after the president's rejection of Jonathan's petition. He responded that he wasn't given a chance to ask a question.

As I related the incident to my congregation the following Shabbat, I said in exasperation, "Whatever the protocol, if one cares enough about the issue, shouldn't you jump to your feet and say, 'Mr. President, we protest your handling of the Jonathan Pollard case.'?" A close friend called out, "That's why you're not invited to such meetings!"

But if the price of such invitations is to compromise on the truth, then I prefer to stand outside the gates. My voice is much louder and truer from there.

July 1995

Principle Thirty-Three

The Welfare of Demonstrators
Takes Precedence Over the Cause Itself

A cornerstone of my activism is the principle that the cause, no matter how just, never outweighs a leader's primary responsibility to his or her supporters. Demonstrators have an absolute right to be made fully aware in advance of what is being planned. Moreover, if participants in a demonstration find themselves in danger, the leader of the group should immediately terminate the action. The safety of the participants must come first.

Incensed by what I perceived as Jimmy Carter's pronounced tilt toward the Arabs throughout his presidency, I asked my students at Stern College for Women of Yeshiva University to join me in protest against Carter's reelection as president in 1980. Scores of my women students showed up with me outside a New York hotel where he was addressing an election rally.

It proved to be a frightening experience. Immediately upon our arrival, New York police roughly shoved us behind barriers, separating us from those entering the hotel to hear the president. Shortly thereafter, the late Rabbi Meir Kahane arrived and carefully took up a position in front of our group. Then, shouting anti-Carter slogans, Rabbi Kahane began pushing hard against the barricade, finally breaking through. Believing that my students were with Rabbi Kahane, the police rushed the entire group, injuring several young women in the process.

Amid the chaos and recriminations of that bitter day, there emerged a fundamental difference between my philosophy of activism and that of Rabbi Kahane. For Rabbi Kahane, it was acceptable not to fully inform his fellow demonstrators of tactics planned if withholding such vital information could serve what he felt were the needs of the Jewish community. The police melee that evening outside the hotel where Carter spoke was caused by Rabbi Kahane's successful effort to deceive the police into believing that my students were joining him in his attempt to storm the barricade. As he revealed that evening and on other occasions, Rabbi Kahane was prepared to place demonstrators at risk if the resultant mayhem served what he believed to be the larger cause.

I strongly disagree with this approach. A cornerstone of my activism is the principle that the cause, no matter how just, never outweighs a leader's primary responsibility to his or her supporters. Demonstrators have an absolute right to be made fully aware in advance of what is being planned. Moreover, if participants find themselves in danger, the leader of the group should immediately terminate the action. The safety of participants must come first. From this perspective, I seriously erred on that evening in 1980 by not sizing up the situation quickly enough and insisting to my followers that we leave the demonstration site as soon as Rabbi Kahane began pushing forward.

This does not mean that if protesters are fully informed of the plans for and possible consequences of a demonstration or act of civil disobedience, they do not then have the right to step forward and place themselves in danger. They do have that right. On countless occasions in cities around the world we organized nonviolent protests that placed participants in danger, sometimes leading to our being beaten or arrested. In each of these situations, however, those who decided to stand with us accepted the risks. But even in these cases, only people old enough to make mature choices were allowed to participate.

Aside from being made fully aware of the type of demonstration being carried out, participants should be knowledgeable about the issue prompting the protest action. There is a danger that people can be easily swept along into joining a demonstration by the attendant sense of excitement and even glamor. This potential is all the more reason why leaders have the responsibility of insisting that those involved in raising a voice of conscience know the facts. Knowledge is the cornerstone of spiritual activism. No one should engage in activist pursuits unless he or she fully understands and concurs with the position that is being advocated.

Even when knowledgeable, it often occurs that participants, especially students, are used as props. It is common practice to bring students out in busloads to beef up numbers at a rally. That's fine. But things get out of hand when speakers talk as if the students were not there, speaking over their heads, or not engaging them in ways that are meaningful and educational. When this occurs students begin to mill around, socialize, and banter. They're the first to recognize when they're being used.

Some who have insisted that the cause must take precedence over everything else, have cited the Jewish tradition regarding war as evidence of the *halachic* correctness of their position. After all, they argue, in times of war individuals are sacrificed for the welfare of the collective. Why should social action be any different?

Setting aside the point that the Torah shows tremendous sensitivity for each soldier in battle—a soldier who feels uncertain about the reason he is being asked to fight may, according to some opinions, conscientiously object and avoid service—the comparison is fundamentally flawed. War is declared by the government as representative of the entire people, and it therefore becomes a communal obligation for individuals to abide by the government's dictates. On the other hand, a decision as to whether to take part in social action is dictated by personal choice. Every individual makes his or her personal decision whether to become involved.

Note the comment of Nachmanides (Ramban) on the Torah's mandate to count the Jewish people. He emphasizes the Torah's command that each individual be counted separately. Unlike in America, where a census is quantitative and where individuals become numbers and their names are secondary, in Judaism every individual counted is given unique importance and is irreplaceable.

It is for this reason that I have adapted the principle that no matter how righteous a cause may be and no matter how valuable a particular protest action may seem in achieving the aims of that cause, a leader's first responsibility must always be to his fellow demonstrators—even at the expense of the demonstration.

October 2000

Principle Thirty-Four

Respect the Other

An essential principle of the activism that I've been struggling to promulgate is the recognition that no single person has the monopoly on the truth. Whereas most people associate activism with a rigid single-mindedness of purpose and even intolerance, it is my position that although the activist may be committed to a particular cause, he or she must be open and respectful of dissenting views.

Outside the New York synagogue where Rabbi Yehuda Amital (the only Orthodox rabbi in Prime Minister Shimon Peres' cabinet) was scheduled to speak some weeks ago, several supporters of the Israeli political right respectfully distributed flyers listing suggested questions about the peace process.

Virtually everyone who entered the synagogue accepted the flyers—with one major exception. A prominent New York rabbi from the West Side took the piece of paper, glanced at it, and proceeded to rip it up. In explaining his action to the individual who had handed him the flyer, he declared emphatically that dissent had no place in this setting. It was not even the nature or content of the dissent that provoked his action; rather he was protesting the very existence of dissent. Of course he had every right to do so; he is free to dissent against dissent. Such are the benefits of living in a free society. Still, as a proponent of activism based on Jewish spiritual values, I found his reaction deeply disturbing.

An essential principle of the activism that I've been struggling to promulgate is the recognition that no single person has the monopoly on truth. Whereas most people associate activism with a rigid single-mindedness of purpose and even intolerance, it is my position that although the activist may be committed to a particular cause, he or she must be open and respectful of dissenting views.

Activists convinced of the righteousness of their positions must also acknowledge the spiritual value and goodness of those with whom they disagree. It is not for naught that page after page of the Talmud records two and sometimes three or more opinions on a single issue. In doing so, the Talmud teaches us that divergent views must be respected and given a proper hearing. Even opinions that rabbis ultimately rejected are mentioned in the text. What is rejected today may be adopted another day, the Talmud notes. By listening to the views of others, one might come to accept elements of another's thinking and use them to reshape one's own.

I first came to understand this principle of listening through my dealings with the far right wing of the Gush Emunim movement. On one occasion, during those years when I strongly believed that Israel should incorporate Judea and Samaria, I had a meeting with one of the settlement movement's most prominent leaders, Rabbi Moshe Levinger. Rabbi Levinger did virtually all of the talking. Even when I did succeed in interjecting a few words, it was clear from his comments that he had not listened to me at all. That experience was so jarring for me that it inspired me to question whether, in my Jewish activism, I too was guilty of not listening.

The propensity to not listen, to discourage and stifle dissent, is by no means the exclusive characteristic of the right. At times some of the most liberal and reputedly most tolerant voices in the Jewish community are equally guilty of refusing to listen.

In the fall of 1992, for example, I vigorously protested former New York City mayor David Dinkins' handling of the Yankele Rosenbaum case. Dinkins was the scheduled speaker at the Jewish

Theological Seminary (JTS) in New York. From my seat in the front row, I rose to shake Dinkins' hand as he entered the auditorium. This was my way of communicating to him, in my mind at least, that the conflict was not a personal one.

Throughout his talk, however, and particularly when criticizing some in the clergy for inflaming racial tensions, Dinkins, as the *New York Post* described it the next day, "stared directly at Rabbi Avi Weiss, one of his harshest critics in the case." When Dinkins completed his talk, JTS Chancellor Ismar Schorsch, who was chairing the event, invited questions from the audience. Rabbi Schorsch obviously saw my raised hand, a clear indication to him that I had no intention of disrupting the proceedings. However, he refused to acknowledge me. He knew I disagreed with the mayor and therefore my views could not be tolerated. For good measure, the next day *New York Newsday* quoted him as labeling me "the Jewish Al Sharpton."

Both Rabbi Schorsch and Rabbi Levinger refused to listen. In their intolerance to hearing the views of others, they were indistinguishable.

Judaic principles demand that we hear each other. No wonder that when the prophet Malachi talks about positive speech he uses the passive voice: *Az nidberu yirai Hashem ish el rei'eihu*, "Then the God-fearing were spoken to, each to the other." He does so to stress the principle that hearing is at least as important as speaking.

Hearing—listening—is something that the West Side rabbi who tore up the flyer refused to do. He refused to accept the principle that in the realm of respecting others, the real challenge is not listening to those who agree with us, but listening to those who do not.

May 1996

THE AFTERMATH

The Spiritual Activist appreciates that there are consequences to activism, including the need to deal with anger and criticism, as well as the need to reassess the issues being dealt with.

The Spiritual Activist acknowledges limitations, is prepared to be self-critical, and recognizes that even in success there can be a downside.

The Spiritual Activist never despairs while understanding that goals are not achieved all at once.

Principle Thirty-Five

Deal with Anger and Criticism
while Operating from the Fringe

Anger can energize people to act more passionately and more powerfully. But it must be remembered that anger consumes a great deal of energy—and all of us, even the youngest and most ardent among us, have limits to our energy. The energy we possess should be used constructively rather than expended destructively, in ineffective fury and rage.

The spiritual activism with which I have been involved has taken place, by and large, on the fringe. This is not to imply that those who operate within the establishment do not contribute. They, of course, can and often do. Yet I have always felt that it is from the fringe that one has the independence to carve out a mission and to follow through with a plan of action.

This "fringe" strategy, however, almost inevitably leads to one major consequence. Those who work within the establishment tend to be not at all happy with those outside the inner circle who initiate and carry through campaigns of their own. Often in my years of activism, I have found myself locked out by those who operate from within, and occasionally even dealt with in ways that can only be described as humiliating. And often, too, such treatment has aroused my anger, with which I have had to learn how to cope, as I have had to learn how to deal with the criticism that my activism has at times provoked.

In the fall of 1992, for example, during the period when I was strongly critical of then New York City Mayor David Dinkins' handling of the Yankele Rosenbaum case, the mayor was scheduled to speak at the General Assembly of the Council of Jewish Federations. As I entered the hotel lobby where he was to give his address, I was stunned when two New York City detectives accosted me. I immediately recognized one of them, who was the same detective who had been assigned to protect me when my life had been threatened following the assassination of Rabbi Meir Kahane. I will never forget what he said to me. "I'm embarrassed, Avi," the detective said. "I'll be with you all evening on the instructions of the Assembly leadership. My task is not to protect you from others, but to protect David Dinkins from you."

Two years later, I attended another General Assembly in Denver. A couple of weeks earlier, I had sent a letter to Council of Jewish Federation leaders requesting that the case of Jonathan Pollard be discussed in a plenary session. The request was turned down. On the evening that Prime Minister Yitzhak Rabin was to address the Assembly, I was singled out from an audience of over two thousand people by several security agents and escorted out of the room. They advised me that they were acting on instructions from General Assembly leadership. Throngs of people were entering the auditorium as I was being led away in humiliation, the dictum "to publicly embarrass someone is like shedding blood" running through my mind. No apologies or explanations were ever offered.

There were many other similar affronts. But the event that probably hurt the most occurred when the establishment National Conference of Soviet Jewry and the activist Student Struggle for Soviet Jewry which I chaired, sent representatives to Helsinki in May of 1989. Both our groups had gone there to raise a voice for Soviet Jewry during President Reagan's visit to Helsinki on his way to Moscow for a summit with Soviet President Mikhail Gorbachev. On the night of our arrival, the National Conference hosted an address by former Secretary of State George Schultz at a local synagogue. As I moved toward the synagogue, guards were waiting for me at the gate. "You're Rabbi Weiss, " one of them said. "We've been waiting for you and are under strict orders not to let you in." I was taken aback. Young people often volunteered to protect our group when we traveled to different European cities, on behalf of the Jewish people. And here stood young people, with orders to block my entrance. I sent a personal note to a conference official I knew through one of the guards. "It's cold outside," I wrote. "Don't humiliate me by locking me out." No response ever came. Nor did any apology.

While this litany of humiliations from the fringe might, on the surface, sound like a somewhat embittered attempt to air old grievances, I offer it here because I am convinced that an important principle of spiritual activism can be derived from it. I admit that in moments such as the ones that I have described I have been not only embarrassed and hurt, but also deeply angry. Over the years, however, I have developed a way to deal with the kind of abuse those of us on the fringe sometimes incur from those on the inside, as well as with the personal anger that often ensues from being subjected to such treatment.

It must be realized and accepted that anger is an emotion, a feeling that just is. We cannot control what we feel. We can, however, control what we do. This, then, constitutes the first challenge: Because one feels angry does not mean that one must act angry.

To be sure, anger can energize people to act more passionately and more powerfully. But, and this is our second challenge, it must be remembered that anger consumes a great deal of energy-and all of us, even the youngest and most ardent among us, have limits to our energy. The energy we possess should be used constructively rather than expended destructively, in ineffective fury and rage.

Like anger, the criticism that comes inevitably from those who disagree with our mode of operation must also be dealt with. The first step is to assess whether such criticism is coming from someone we respect, someone who truly cares about us and whose criticism is therefore sincerely offered in our interest. If this is so, then the rule of the spiritual activist should be to seriously take that criticism into account. Criticism at its best should prompt, if necessary, a serious reassessment and re-evaluation of one's actions.

But when the criticism comes from sources that do not have our best interests at heart, we must simply endure it and move on. Indeed, if we conclude that our actions were justified, we continue with our struggle according to our own lights. A deep and passionate belief in the cause is the animating quality for the spiritual activist and the cornerstone of success. The activist who believes powerfully in what he or she is doing will, despite occasional humiliations, be able to channel anger and move forward in the face of criticism. A solid and unwavering belief in one's cause is the seed and origin of all great accomplishment.

May 2001

Principle Thirty-Six

Seek Consensus in Israel

Toward the end of the Passover seder, we sing songs of redemption. One of these songs expresses a longing for the time when "a day will come that will be neither day nor night." I never understood what this line meant until now. Now I know that it expresses a yearning for twilight in Israel that will no longer be fleeting. In twilight we will find consensus, the roadway to peace.

Twilight is "fleeting" in the Holy Land, writes Herbert Weiner in *The Wild Goats of Ein Gedi.* "The bright red sun drops swiftly into the Mediterranen, and it is sudden and complete night…Might this either-or mood of the land have something to do with the harsh polarized extremism of its prophets?"

Some suggest that the land reflects the politics of its people. In Israeli politics it's either day or night—a country of extremes divided between right and left.

This politically charged atmosphere pervades Israeli life. I vividly recall my experience this past summer at Shaare Zedek Hospital in Jerusalem after I suffered a heart attack while protesting a terrorist bombing in Jerusalem. It was a frightening time. There I was, worried about my health, when I realized that the doctors surrounding me were engaged in a heated political debate. I remember wondering, With one supporting Labor and the other Likud, would they remember that it was the right coronary and not the left anterior descending that needed repair?

But that's the way it is in Israel. Almost everyone has precise, defined and hard-nosed political opinions.

Consider language. Some on the right shouted, "Rabin is a traitor" when, as prime minister, he negotiated with the PLO. Some on the left called Menachem Begin a murderer during the Lebanon War.

Consider each side's attempt to delegitimize the other. Too many on the right believe that when the government is wrong, it is illegal—a sure prescription for anarchy. Too many on the left refer to Israeli settlers as "implants." Even Yitzhak Rabin, of blessed memory, once suggested that Israel need only defend the ninety-seven percent of its citizenry who lived within the Green Line, not the three percent who live in Judea and Samaria.

Consider Israel's history of Jew killing Jew. The late prime minister David Ben Gurion ordered the attack on the Altalena, an Irgun ship loaded with munitions on its way to Israel. Now the catastrophe of catastrophes, Rabin has been murdered by an Orthodox, yarmulke-wearing Jew.

It is time for extreme politics to make way for the politics of consensus. As painful as it is for those like myself who have debated and written about the propriety of Israel incorporating Judea and Samaria, we must now recognize that the withdrawal of Israeli troops from seven cities in Israel's heartland means that the philosophy of "Not One Inch" no longer reflects political reality. The left must likewise recognize that uprooting settlers and settlements cotravenes the will of the people. A compromise map should be drawn up whereby ninety-five percent of Palestinians living in Judea and Samaria will remain in a Palestinian entity, while ninety-five percent of settlers will remain under Israeli rule.

The challenge facing Prime Minister Shimon Peres is to build a government based on compromise and common ground. Will his government adopt the policies of the extreme and give up the Golan, parts of Jerusalem and all of Judea and Samaria, creating a Palestinian state? Or will it practice consensus politics?

There is another area in which the politics of consensus must be adopted. The government must recognize that the opposition has a role to play in Israeli politics. This is especially true in light of the fact that Knesset support for the Oslo II agreement with the PLO was limited to a narrow 61-59 vote.

Israeli democracy could learn from the American democratic system. The framers of the U.S. Constitution insisted that momentous decisions such as declaring war and signing treaties must be ratified by a two-thirds majority. In Israel, as in the United States, fifty-one percent of the legislature should not be enough to approve an accord with such significant consequences as Oslo II. But that is the law as it exists in Israel today.

Given the razor-thin margin, one would expect the government to reach out to the minority, listening closely to its positions. Sadly, however, many Labor leaders have adopted the posture of Interior Minister Haim Ramon, who declared on ABC's "Nightline" a few weeks ago that democracy means that the minority must go along with the majority or else it will be "crushed." We will never be able to make peace with our enemies if we do not first make peace among ourselves.

Toward the end of the Passover seder, we sing songs of redemption. One of these songs expresses a longing for the time when "a day will come that will be neither day nor night." I never understood what this line meant until now. Now I know that it expresses a yearning for twilight in Israel that will no longer be fleeting. In twilight we will find consensus, the roadway to peace.

January 1996

Principle Thirty-Seven

Be Able to Criticize Oneself and One's Movement in Front of One's Own Constituents

The central challenge today is to bring Jews together. Both right and left must stop the finger-pointing that has continued unabated since the assassination. If these recriminations continue, the catastrophe of Rabin's murder will pale next to the catastrophe ahead. Instead, each side should look inward and seek to put its own house in order.

Grief stricken upon hearing that Prime Minister Yitzhak Rabin had been murdered, I made my way to the Israeli consulate in New York to participate in a hastily called memorial service. As I joined the crowd, a supporter of the peace process shouted, "Avi, shame! Your people murdered the prime minister! His blood is on your hands!" Others called out, "Your words are responsible for the assassination! Go home!"

I thought of the countless times members of fringe groups would shout, "Rabin is a traitor" at right-wing rallies I attended. I would always declare that invective of this sort is not to be tolerated. To this, they would at times chant, "Weiss is a traitor!"

As unwelcome as I felt at the consulate, I did not go home, for as a religious Zionist I believe that the post of prime minister of Israel has spiritual significance. Rav Avraham Yitzhak HaKohen Kook wrote that the head of the Jewish state has the status of a biblical king. Thus when Rabin was murdered, the very soul of the state, which his leadership embodied, was also extinguished. He was prime minister of all our people—those who agreed with his policies and those, like myself, who disagreed.

As I held a memorial candle for the prime minister, I was also mourning the division that had ripped our community apart. If a Jew can lift a gun to assassinate the prime minister of Israel, we are perhaps only a hairbreadth away from Jews confronting other Jews in a civil war. This would be the end of the Zionist dream.

Civil war is indeed possible. While the responsible right has disagreed with but never delegitimized the government, those on the fringe right have taken the position that when the government is wrong it is illegitimate. For these misguided individuals, it follows that they have the right to do what their perverted view of Jewish law demands—including taking up arms against the enemy, even if the "enemy" is Israel's prime minister.

The central challenge today is to bring Jews together. Both right and left must stop the finger-pointing that has continued unabated since the assassination. If these recriminations continue, the catastrophe of Rabin's murder will pale next to the catastrophe ahead. Instead, each side should look inward and seek to put its own house in order.

Specifically, the right must understand that slogans such as "Rabin is a traitor" or acts such as burning Rabin in effigy are despicable. The left must recognize that to characterize those opposed to the peace process as "collaborators with Hamas" is equally malicious. Such slogans echo those heard after Sabra and Shatilla when former prime minister Menachem Begin was called "murderer of children."

Speaking from the right, I must strongly agree with Leah Rabin that those who labeled her husband a murderer may have created a climate that allowed the assassin to commit his crime. But Mrs. Rabin's own party should take issue with her for charging the Likud and its leader, Benjamin Netanyahu, with having blood on their hands. Both sides must recognize that while a word is a word and a deed is a deed, words lead to deeds.

Just as right and left must be careful with language, so each must recognize that it does not possess the only true answers for achieving peace. Those who oppose trading land for peace must understand that they have no monopoly on loving all the land of Israel: Yitzhak Rabin loved the land as much as any of them. Similarly, those who support the peace process must understand that they have no monopoly on wanting peace. The right yearns for peace as much as does the left, but the right has serious problems with *this* peace process, which even President Ezer Weizman has called "a bloody process."

There is one more area in which both sides need self-examination. The right must condemn those on its fringe whose grasp of *halakhah* is simplistic. The assassin's claim that he acted in accordance with God's wishes has no place in the complex halakhic system. It does not have a scintilla of support in Torah and is the distorted view of those on the extreme edge. Similarly, the left must shun the simplistic grouping of all those on the political right with the extreme right fringe. Judaism rejects collective guilt and punishment. We cannot allow the evil of the extremes to turn us against the good of the vast majority in the moderate center.

Rav Kook pointed out that the Second Temple was destroyed because of gratuitous hatred. It will be rebuilt, he said, when the hate is replaced with love. A starting point would be for each of us to look into our own souls. We must recognize that the test of love is not how we respect those who agree with us, but how we respect those who do not.

December 1995

Principle Thirty-Eight

Every Struggle Has Its Price

As in everything, there is no absolute good. Every step forward always contains the possibility of unforeseen problems. The Swiss story is no different. In the process of focusing so mightily on monies, we must also be vigilant against the danger that this preoccupation might take precedence over, perhaps even eclipse, what must always remain the predominant memory—the murder of the Six Million.

Recouping monies and plundered assets deposited in Swiss banks and elsewhere has taken center stage in the saga of Shoah memory. There is absolutely no doubt that every dime should be recovered. But, as in everything, there is no absolute good. Every step forward always contains the possibility of unforeseen problems. The Swiss story is no different. In the process of focusing so mightily on monies, we must also be vigilant against the danger that this preoccupation might take precedence over, perhaps even eclipse, what must always remain the predominant memory—the murder of the Six Million.

Shoah memory has gone through several stages of bereavement, which follow the general pattern of the Jewish tradition of mourning.

For the first twenty years after the Shoah, survivors, and for that matter the larger Jewish community, were silent. For example, many rabbis teaching at my yeshiva high school in the late 1950s and early 1960s were survivors, yet never once did I hear any mention of the Shoah.

Shoah memory lay dormant for many reasons. Survivors were still shell-shocked from the horror of horrors. So preoccupied were they with picking up the pieces of their lives and moving on, so overwhelming was the task facing them, that there was little energy for anything else. Moreover, for many survivors, what they had endured was so humiliating that they were unable to speak about their experiences. It must also be said that many of us were unwilling at the time, for a vast array of reasons, to listen to their stories. Those years resembled a protracted observance of the Jewish mourning period of *aninut*—that period of time between death and burial in which the bereaved are considered to be so traumatized that Jewish law exempts them from the performance of any of the commandments.

It took about twenty years, until about the time of the Six Day War, for the community of Israel to begin a collective *shivah* process, the seven-day period of reflection during which the bereaved begin to take stock of the memory of the departed, and during which those who come to comfort them attend to their tales. It was at this time that Holocaust studies began to evolve and be legitimized in the culture at large. So powerful was Shoah memory then that for many Jews Judaism became—and unfortunately for some still remains—a branch of the Holocaust rather than the Holocaust being subsumed within Judaism.

This process of memory reached its crescendo in 1978 when the U.S. government announced a plan to support the building of the Holocaust Memorial Museum on federal land. Shoah memory was "in"; the past was finally being remembered in a profound and detailed way.

By 1985 the Jewish community in America began to face a new phenomenon—Holocaust revisionism. Although the process had started years earlier, it had been marginal. During the mid-1980s, however, revisionism burst into the public eye. President Ronald Reagan was an unwitting participant when he made the terrible mistake of going to Bitburg, thereby declaring a moral equivalency between the Waffen SS and the victims. Pope John Paul II in 1987 embraced President Kurt Waldheim of Austria, an unrepentant Nazi, calling him a "prince of peace." The convent at Auschwitz was another form of revisionism, seen by some as an attempt to Christianize the Shoah. In addition, Holocaust deniers shamelessly escalated the dissemination of their lies and calumnies.

Fifty years after the Shoah, the period of what can be called "short-term memory" was concluded. Anniversary ceremonies commemorating the fiftieth anniversary of liberation were conducted. While survivors viewed such events as an indication that the world had at last acknowledged their suffering, others, like the governments and many individuals in Germany, Poland, and Austria hoped that the ceremonies would serve as a last chapter in the memory process, a way finally to be rid of the memory of the Shoah that tainted them so profoundly.

Today we are moving from "short-term memory" to "long-term memory." How the Shoah will be remembered into the future very much depends on how we treat this transition period, a period that sets the tone for future memory, casting its shadow forward.

Herein lies my concern. As in the normal grieving process, during which estates have to be put in order and the business of the dead must be concluded, today our community has focused upon the details of recovering assets. No doubt this process will take decades. What price will this extract from Shoah memory? What will be the ramifications if Jews and Jewish organizations begin to quarrel over unclaimed funds? What will happen to the larger percentage of survivors who didn't lose money but claim that they suffered no less, and feel that they are being ignored? What would happen to Shoah memory if it were discovered that not only did the Swiss steal but some Jews also stole money from other Jews, illegally removing Jewish funds from bank accounts.

I am the first to applaud the courage of those who have dedicated themselves to winning financial restitution for Holocaust survivors, but I am deeply concerned that as this effort continues, the sacred essence of Holocaust memory may be compromised. Indeed, many involved in recovering funds have said precious little about Holocaust revisionism.

As we move into the stage of "long-term memory," the key challenge is to preserve the truth about the Holocaust even as we pursue the just return of funds. If we do not meet this challenge, there is a real danger that the Holocaust will be remembered for stolen money rather than stolen souls.

May 1997

Principle Thirty-Nine

Never Despair

Yet even with the knife dangling over Jerusalem and our people, we have faith that ultimately it will be lifted and disaster will be averted. More than ever, Jerusalem reflects God's promise to remain with us. God's covenant with Abraham and with Jerusalem, no matter the obstacles, forever endures. The multifaceted richness of the city, its political, emotional, and spiritual faces reflecting the human complexity of its founder, the majestic King David, reminds us to never despair, never give up.

Almost alone among cities, Jerusalem transcends its physical essence to reach exalted spiritual and metaphorical levels. The many faces of Jerusalem are reflected in the rich and complex personality of King David who established his sovereignty there. As Rabbi David Silber, the great teacher of Bible notes, there is the David of the Book of Samuel, the David of the Book of Psalms and the David of our liturgy. Corresponding to these three aspects of this monumental king, there is the political Jerusalem, the loving Jerusalem, and the Jerusalem of eternal spiritual transcendence.

In the Book of Samuel, David is portrayed as a strong and pragmatic political figure who, to protect his kingship, does everything in his power to keep the people of Israel together. He fends off the rebellion of his son Absalom, prevents Sheva ben Bichri from separating the ten tribes from the realm, and in his later years quashes the revolt of his son Adoniyah.

Not coincidentally, the Jerusalem that David establishes as the capital of Israel is situated between the tribes of Benjamin in the north and Judah in the south, bridging, in effect, the enmity between the House of Saul and the House of David. In the Book of Genesis, Judah, in his most sublime moment, rises to tell his father Jacob that he would guarantee the safety of his brother Benjamin, his de-facto rival for the birthright and sovereignty with Joseph out of the picture. And if I fail, Judah concludes with extraordinary nobility, "I will have sinned to you all of my days."

In a similar fashion, Jerusalem turns adversaries into friends, sending the message that unity is the way to survival. Its very name-Yeru, the city of shalem, unity-proclaims that notwithstanding our differences, we must acknowledge our oneness and learn to love one another. Like a dove that can fly only with both wings on an even plane reaching out in opposite directions, so too, only through the cooperative efforts of opposing forces- religious and nonreligious, right and left-can Jerusalem soar.

Beyond its practical, earthly manifestation, Jerusalem is endowed with powerful lyrical, romantic, loving qualities like those reflected in the Book of Psalms. In poem after poem, King David expresses his yearning for God's embrace. "Though I walk in the valley of the shadow of death I fear no evil, for You o God are with me," he declares. "Though my father and mother have left me, the Lord Will gather in me," he sings, articulating his limitless love for God equaled only by God's limitless love for him.

Jerusalem, similarly, is described in tender, protective terms-in the words of King David, "Jerusalem, hills surround it." Like the bride who circles the groom and the groom who places a ring on his bride's finger, the hills encircle Jerusalem like a ring that reflects God's love and protection of the city in which He resides. Circular imagery suggests protectiveness and embrace, the intimacy of figures who cannot live without each other-an intimacy in which one loves deeply and feels deeply loved in return.

And so, under the wedding canopy we declare, "May there

soon be heard in the streets of Jerusalem the sounds of joy and gladness, the voice of the groom and the voice of the bride." Jerusalem is evoked as the city of love-of God's love as well as of the most intimate human love. The name of its first king, David, means beloved. And while commentaries compare David to Joseph, the latter, as Rabbi Silber points out, was despised by many, whereas David, even in times of woe and vexation, seems always to have been beloved.

Like David, Jerusalem remains the emotional center, the beloved heart of our people even in the most troubled times. Today we desperately feel the need for God's embrace. The situation is so perilous that we are not even sure what to pray for. All we can do is stand before the Merciful One and allow Him to guide us to pray for what we need. We lean on the Lord. In the words of the Psalmist, we "trust in His kindness," words that Rabbi Shlomo Carlebach interpreted to mean that even before we are helped, even when it is still dark, we have faith that God will pull us through.

Jerusalem, much like the beloved, always remains in some measure beyond our grasp, always a metaphor to aspire to. It is a city that eternally awaits completion; it is forever in a state of becoming, of process, of spiritual transformation and transcendence, like the David of the liturgy. "And to Jerusalem your city return in mercy, " we pray. Jerusalem represents dreams seeking fulfillment, process eternally seeking completion. Though it was not David who built the Temple but his son Solomon, its dedication is linked to the father as he was the one who introduced the idea, he was the one with the original vision even if he never saw it to fruition.

Eternally elusive, like a vision or dream longing for fulfillment, Jerusalem is today in great danger. The dagger of the enemy hovers over it as Abraham's knife hovered over his son Isaac's neck on Mount Moriah in the heart of the city, and as the angel of death's knife threatened the city as is recounted in the closing chapter of

Samuel II, and only at the last moment did God have it lifted. Today suicide bombers target the holy city. On a recent solidarity mission to Israel, we too experienced the proximity of terror when a member of our group was lightly injured at the Sbarro's restaurant and his niece whom he had invited to lunch was critically wounded and today lies close to death. Jerusalem in all of its faces is under siege.

Yet even with the knife dangling over Jerusalem and our people, we have faith that ultimately it will be lifted and disaster will be averted. More than ever, Jerusalem reflects God's promise to remain with us. God's covenant with Abraham and with Jerusalem, no matter the obstacles, forever endures. The multifaceted richness of the city, its political, emotional, and spiritual faces reflecting the human complexity of its founder, the majestic King David, reminds us to never despair, never give up. In the words of the Psalmist incorporated into the liturgy, the ultimate restoration of Jerusalem in all of its tangible, tender and transcendent forms is assured: "The Lord builds Jerusalem. He gathers in the dispersed of Israel. He heals the brokenhearted, and mends their wounds."

August 2001

Principle Forty

The False Messianism of Quick Fix Solutions

It is a natural and understandable yearning by very good people on both sides to dispel the darkness of the Shoah with the fulfillment of the messianic dream of land or of peace. But true messianism is, in reality, a movement that is in constant process. The rabbis liken the messianic era to the rising of the sun; it happens in stages, gradually—in rabbinic terms, "*kim 'ah, kim'ah.*"

Once again we are living in an era of false messiahs. Judaism has had a long and sorrowful list of "salvations" in the past that have gone awry. Not coincidentally, each of these misguided movements appeared in the wake of tragic times for our people when the only hope seemed to be the emergence of a leader who would turn everything around—a savior who would usher in the redemption.

After the destruction of the Second Temple, the great Rabbi Akiva considered Bar Kochba such a leader. Shabbetai Tzvi was hailed as a messiah in the seventeenth century as the decrees of the notorious Jew-killer Bogdan Chmelnicki took hold.

The darkest period in Jewish history—the Shoah—occurred in our own time, and it too has produced a variety of messianic movements, redemptive in nature, each emphasizing that salvation must come now and cannot wait.

Two of these movements centered in Israel, Gush Emunim and Peace Now, ironically on opposite ends of the political spectrum, are nevertheless profoundly akin in spirit because of their essentially messianic nature, and above all because they are, ultimately, cautionary examples of false messianism.

The Gush Emunim movement gained force in the sixties after the Six Day War, a period also characterized by a new readiness to openly confront the tragedy of the Shoah. The movement maintained that the entirety of Judea, Samaria and Gaza captured in that war should immediately be incorporated into "Greater Israel" as the time of the Messiah was at hand. Though energized by idealistic leaders, it did not bring the Messiah.

Peace Now, or Shalom Achshav, despite its pragmatic and secular assertions, is also fundamentally messianic at its core. The emphasis on the word "Now" testifies to a deep messianic urgency, a profound faith in the promise of the imminence of peace. However, the "quick fix" of peace that its well-intentioned leaders envisioned still eludes us. It is also a false dream—another false messiah.

There was a time when the political left in Israel argued that the right was made up of messianists whose heads were in the clouds as they militated to liberate every inch of biblical Israel. Now the tables have turned. It is the right that turns to the left and suggests that they are the messianists with their heads in the clouds for insisting that peace is at hand.

It is a natural and understandable yearning by very good people on both sides to dispel the darkness of the Shoah with the fulfillment of the messianic dream of land or of peace. But true messianism is, in reality, a movement that is in constant process. The rabbis liken the messianic era to the rising of the sun; it happens in stages, gradually—in rabbinic terms, *"kim'ah, kim'ah."*

Gush Emunim must now acknowledge that the idea of incorporating all of Judea, Samaria and Gaza is folly and unrealistic because of the presence of an Arab majority that cannot be ignored; it is a false messiah. Similarly, Peace Now must recognize that the hope for immediate peace is also a false messiah. The ongoing demonization and terrorizing of Israel by the Arabs reflects an unwillingness for real peace. The imposition of peace with such a partner would clearly be enormously dangerous to the security and future well-being of Israel.

There is a rabbinic tradition that maintains that the Messiah will be born on the ninth day of Av, the day on which we commemorate the destruction of both Temples. One way of interpreting this tradition is as a warning that it is precisely in the most difficult times that we are prone to believe that the Messiah will soon be arriving; so desperate is the situation that the only way out is for the Messiah to come immediately without a moment to spare.

Today, when Israel is again vulnerable and threatened, we continue to pray and work for the arrival of the Messiah, but we must recognize that there are no quick fixes. Instant solutions which belie the complexity of a situation we all hope will soon end in a true and lasting peace, are nothing less than false promises. They are false messiahs which can lead to even greater tragedy and disappointment, and against which we must all be on guard.

January 2001

Principle Forty-One

After September 11:
Love of America Does Not Preclude Love of Israel

The magnitude of the September 11 events is so enormous that one hesitates to even bring up the concerns of one's own religious or ethnic group, yet I cannot help but feel that my government is placing a lesser value on the sufferings of people who are, like myself, both Americans and Jews.

In the makeshift morgue at "ground zero," near the wreckage of the World Trade Center, I stood with several priests as a double line of rescue workers formed to honor the remains of a police officer being borne in. We, the members of the clergy, snapped to attention together with the firefighters and the dead man's comrades on the police force. As they saluted, we placed our hands over our hearts. It was a holy moment as clergy of different faiths gave respect to one who had lost his life in the act of trying to save the lives of others. It was a moment that reflected the strong sense of a shared vulnerability and destiny that many of us have been feeling in recent days as Americans and as citizens of the world community.

As a rabbi, I experienced this as what can be called a "Bereishit" or "Genesis" moment. The Torah, begins not with a story particular to the Jewish people, but with the universal story of creation. When God created the world, all of the earth was created, not only the land of Israel.

But lately, this feeling of intense closeness to my American identity has been marred when, as a Jew, I witness a distinction being drawn between an acceptable type of terrorism in Israel and the unacceptability of terrorism in all of its manifestations in America. When the leader of my country, President Bush, says concerning the unrest in the Middle East, "We are fully committed to working with both sides to bring the level of terrorism down to an acceptable level for both," (quoted in the New York Post, October 3, 2001) he is telling me, and every member of the American Jewish community, that there is a level of terrorism that is acceptable for Israel whereas no level of terrorism is tolerable in the United States.

The magnitude of the September 11 events is so enormous that one hesitates to even bring up the concerns of one's own religious or ethnic group, yet I cannot help but feel that my government is placing a lesser value on the sufferings of people who are, like myself, both Americans and Jews. Terrorists from Hamas, Hizbollah and Islamic Jihad who have murdered American citizens outside of Israel are on America's most wanted list, yet terrorists from those very same organizations who murdered American citizens in Israel are not on the list. On the one hand, America is relentlessly pursuing Osama bin Laden "dead or alive." On the other hand, the United States is openly critical of Israel for pursuing the terrorists behind the suicide bombing that murdered fifteen Israelis, including an American citizen, at the Sbarro pizza restaurant in Jerusalem this past August.

The irony is that by making distinctions among terrorists the U.S. government not only creates the sense that the lives of some of its citizens are of less value, but it also wreaks havoc with the essential unifying principle that the eradication of all terrorism everywhere without exception is a universal cause in which all just and good people must be enlisted. The only way to fight terrorism here in the United States is to fight it in Afghanistan, in Pakistan, in Syria and all across the entire globe, including in the state that has known for so many years all too well the price and culture of terrorism, Israel. Fighting terrorism in some countries while allowing it in Israel to go unchecked is fatal, for terrorism, as we now know all too well, can and will jump oceans in an instant.

In the wake of September 11, American Jews, while privately deeply worried about the fate of Israel, have by and large remained silent, loath to speak up out of fear of being labeled unpatriotic or of jeopardizing the gathering of the coalition to fight world terrorism. The situation is reminiscent of what occurred during World War II when American Jewish leadership took a deferential role, failing to press the plight of its brothers and sisters in Europe, setting aside its "lesser" concerns in the face of what was deemed as the more urgent "greater" war effort; the results as we now know were catastrophic, with the loss of millions of lives in the Holocaust. Similarly today, the failure to accord equal weight to terrorism in one country gravely undermines the pursuit and eradication of terrorism worldwide, and, moreover, casts the entire enterprise in a morally equivocal and politically expedient light.

During the Cold War, Israel was a bulwark against Soviet expansionism in the Middle East. Today it is the cornerstone against terrorist domination of the world. America must realize that if terrorism is not eradicated in Israel it will never be eradicated in America. As Israeli Prime Minister Ariel Sharon has said, "There is no good terrorism and bad terrorism. We have been fighting terrorism for over one hundred years. Unfortunately, there is no swift and immediate solution. But if we confront this terrorism united, we will be able to overcome it and bring peace. And we shall overcome."

Only together will we overcome, both here on the soil of our beloved land of the free and in the land of our ancient heritage.

October 2001

Closing Reflection: A Personal Note

Coping with Adversity

On the morning after I suffered my first heart attack—a life-altering event that occurred in September 1986 while I was protesting the appearance of the Russian Moiseyev Dance Company at Lincoln Center in New York City—I asked the nurse what time that day I would be able to check out. "Oh no," she responded, "you don't understand. No one leaves the hospital straight from the intensive cardiac-care unit. You first have to go to a regular room to recuperate."

Nine years later it happened again. This time I was stricken while participating in an emotional demonstration in Jerusalem a few hours after two city buses were blown up by Arab terrorists, leaving scores of Israelis dead and wounded.

My doctors told me later that my second heart attack had not been nearly as dangerous as my first, in which the left anterior descent, a key vessel supplying blood to the heart, had completely closed up, leaving no alternative but bypass surgery. The second time around it was the right coronary, a less important artery, that had closed. This time the doctors inserted a stent, a tiny metal piece, which they implanted into the vessel to keep it open.

Yet, from an emotional and psychological perspective, the first attack was easier to handle. As a rabbi more naturally prone toward nurturing and counseling than to confrontation, who has nevertheless willed himself for decades to perform high-profile and high-stakes acts of peaceful civil disobedience, I felt confident that I would similarly be able to overcome my heart condition through the application of will power and concerted effort. Hence my sanguine belief that I would be leaving the hospital the very next day after the first heart attack. And even after undergoing open heart surgery, I was certain I would achieve a full recovery. I vowed to myself that I would exercise, keep the fat and cholesterol down, and all would be well. I was in denial.

During the ensuing years I was involved in some of the most strenuous and dangerous forms of activism I had ever undertaken. I seemed perfectly fine. Yet, after all of these demonstrations, and after faithfully following my doctors' orders for nine years, including exercising regularly and eating the right foods, my heart was stricken a second time. This second attack shattered my confidence as I realized that it was impossible to overcome my condition fully. Suddenly I felt immobilized, like an invalid incapable of getting out of the house.

The year after my second heart attack was probably the most difficult of my life. I felt all was lost. I was a sick man, I thought, and could do nothing to help myself. I began eating the wrong foods, stopped exercising, and soon found myself heavier than I had been in years. By the summer of 1996 I was unable to take even very short walks without feeling angina pain.

My doctor suggested another angiogram. Sure enough, the stent had shut. The procedure had to be done again.

It was during those difficult days, however, that I came to a new understanding of my situation. No longer would I deny my condition or allow myself to be immobilized. I finally relented and accepted the bitter truth that I have cardiac disease. Such is my fate. Yet I also came to recognize that despite my condition, I am not in reality helpless. I am still in a position to change the world.

This idea has a basis in the biblical text, "The number of days in your life I will fulfill." The Talmud understands this to mean that the length of each person's life is decreed by God but can be either added to or subtracted from according to the input of the individual. If I relate this concept to my own situation, it means that I cannot alter the reality that heart disease is part and parcel of my family history. The condition is inherent in my physical being. Yet the Talmud inspires all of us with the awareness that while we cannot fundamentally alter our fate, we are in a position to improve our well being, and add to the length and quality of our lives.

Rav Yosef Dov Soloveitchik, of blessed memory, distinguishes between fate and destiny. Fate capriciously casts each of us into a particular dimension of life that we cannot control. Destiny, on the other hand, "is an active existence in which man confronts the environment into which he was cast....Man is born as an object, dies as an object, but it is within his capacity to live as a subject— as a creator who impresses on his life his individual imprimatur and who lives autonomously." According to Rav Soloveitchik, "Man's mission in this world is to turn fate into destiny, an existence that is passive and influenced to an existence that is active and influential."

Esther Wachsman, whose son Nachshon was kidnapped and killed by Arab terrorists, makes a similar point. "What then is man's purpose and duty in this creation when he is confronted by unexplained tragedy and grief? To withstand, to cope, to deal with the events God sends his way. For none of us has any control over what will happen to us as individuals. What we can control is our reaction, how we deal and how we cope with our grief."

And so on Yom Kippur after what my life-saving cardiologist Dr. Marc Greenberg called the "stent *ha-sheini*" (Hebrew for "second") procedure, I stood before my congregation and for the first time was able to say, "Your rabbi has cardiac disease." These were words I was unable to utter after the first attack. "Nevertheless," I vowed, "this disease will not paralyze me. I have come to understand that the American ideal that there's nothing one can't completely overcome is fallacious. Still, given my limitations and my understanding that I must accept and acknowledge those limitations, I recognize that I still have the capacity to be productive and to accomplish things, albeit in different ways."

The reality is that all of us suffer from some form of limitation—be it physical, intellectual, or psychological—that prevents us from realizing our full potential in our work, family, or personal lives?

We must comprehend the hard truth that limitations are seldom completely vanquished. In contrast to the false sweetness of Hollywood, there are rarely unvarnished happy endings or complete triumphs of willpower. In my own case, I must every day face up to the sobering realization that I will always have cardiac disease. It is not a passing phase. In other words, when doctors tell me to keep stress to a minimum, they mean not only for today but for the rest of my life.

This reality imposes harsh limitations on my ability to live in the manner to which I had become accustomed. But it doesn't mean I cannot empathize with my congregants in time of need. It doesn't mean I must cease speaking out on behalf of oppressed Jewry. What it does mean is that I must temper my actions to take into account my physical limitations even as I continue to act on behalf of those in need of succor.

For this rabbi who has always felt as one with congregants in distress, and for this activist who believes in the importance of going to the point of tension, into the lion's den itself to raise a voice of protest, that is a lifesaving lesson that is not so easily learned or accepted.

Yet my fate and special challenge, especially at moments when I feel limited by my disability, is to remember that in this world there is a kind of "next world" into which one is always graduating. In my case, it is a movement into a realm of activities that is more spiritually demanding and taxing. One can only wonder whether the world of the spirit which has its own pressures, is served by the same heart vessels.

As I move into this new realm, I hear the words of Esther Wachsman ringing in my ears: "One can be a victim of fate or an initiator of new destiny."

A Parable: It's in Our Hands

Once there was a traveling rabbi who had the ability to answer every question. Not once had he ever been wrong. Then one day he arrived at a town where thousands came to hear him. One little girl raised her hand. "I have the question you can't answer," she said. "I have in my hand a bird. Tell me, is this bird alive or dead?"

She was thinking: If the rabbi says the bird is alive, I will close my hand and kill it. If he says the bird is dead, I'll open my hand and let it live.

The rabbi was aware of the trick behind this question, yet still found himself stumped. Here was the question he couldn't answer. Then suddenly the answer hit him. Tears came streaming down his cheeks, even as his face broke into a cherubic smile, much like rain falling in midday sun. He realized he had grasped the secret of Jewish destiny.

Looking at the girl in the midst of the huge crowd, he said: "My precious, precious child. You hold in your hand a bird. You ask if the bird is alive or dead. I can only tell you one thing. The fate of this bird lies in your hands. You can let it live, or you can let it die."

The bird is a metaphor for the Jewish people, for all humankind. It's fate is in our hands, yours and mine. All of us, with the help of God, can make a difference.

Acknowledgments

Central to spiritual activism is the recognition that success requires soul mates— individuals who join together to bring life to our people and all of humankind. In fact, one of the critical tests of leadership is the ability to step back to allow others their rightful sense of ownership, their earned sense of the critical role they play in the effort.

Whatever small success I have had in a variety of areas is due to the companions who have stood with me along the way. Glenn Richter has always been there. A brilliant strategist, he has become my conscience, reminding me always to reach higher. He is indefatigable and of rare integrity—the *tzaddik* of activism. Judy Balint built Coalition for Jewish Concerns/AMCHA into a national organization of twenty thousand strong. She combines absolute commitment to *Am Yisrael* with a deep and sensitive love for others. Rabbi Saul Berman, my rebbe, my friend, has selflessly shared with me his great wisdom which has helped guide me through the years. To these soul mates who have accompanied me on our shared journey, I will always be thankful.

On this journey, my friend and comrade Bernie Glickman has traveled beside me all over the world. His love for Am Yisrael is expressed through his courage and his readiness to take risks, to raise the ultimate voice of Jewish conscience. Hillary Markowitz has been central to our activistic work. Passionate, empathic, Hillary leads the way, teaching others to care, to do for Am Yisrael. Jacob Davidson and Elie Wurtman are two extraordinary men whom I have come to love as family. Mature beyond their years, they have paved the way for young people to realize that they can make a difference. Rabbi Eliot Pearlson, Ronn Torossian, Mike

Zimet, Michael Horen, Robert Kalfus, Gail and Randy Blaustein, Rabbi Pesach Wolicki, Joey Brender, Butch Kahn, Howard Green, Jeffrey Fox, Meredith Weiss and many others have stood with me in the most trying of circumstances. Susie and Vic Alhadeff, Daniel Katz, Hillary and Jeffrey Markowitz, Joe Mermelstein, Dr. Richard Rolnick, Bob Stark, Helene and Norman Stark, Harriet and Marc Suvall, Wendy and John Walls are among the many supporters who made possible the spritual activism of CJC/AMCHA.To all of them, I am eternally grateful.

Over the years I have worked with a few establishment organizations such as the Simon Wiesenthal Center and its leaders. Very special thanks to the World Jewish Congress, which facilitated many of our trips to Europe as we pursued Kurt Waldheim and as we raised a voice against the Christianization of Auschwitz. The heads of the Congress, Rabbi Israel Singer and Elan Steinberg are cherished friends. I will always be grateful to them for their concern and for the long nights they stayed awake to protect us as we faced danger in Poland, Austria, Turkey and Germany.

I am also especially grateful to have met some of the great activists of our generation, especially those heroic Soviet Jews who risked everything to leave the former Soviet Union. Amongst these extraordinary individuals are Yosef Begun, Yosef Mendelevich, Ida Nudel, Avital and Natan Sharansky. To Jacob Birnbaum, the grandfather of the Soviet Jewry movement in America who spoke out with great courage long before it was fashionable, our community owes a great debt of gratitude. And to Pamela Cohen and Micah Naftalin of the Union of Councils for Soviet Jews, as well as Lynn Singer of the Long Island Committee for Soviet Jewry, my deepest blessings for giving so endlessly of themselves and working so closely with the group I chaired, the Student Struggle for Soviet Jewry (SSSJ).

Many lawyers have nobly and selflessly defended us pro bono, among them Alan Dershowitz, who helped us in our suit against Cardinal Joseph Glemp's calumny that we had come to Poland to destroy the convent at Auschwitz and to kill the nuns; Nathan

Lewin, who helped us take the FBI to court after they failed to noti-
fy us until seven months later that I was on Sheikh Rahman's hit
list; Steven Lieberman, who helped us take Howard University to
court for denying us the right to protest on its campus against the
anti-Semite Khalid Muhammad; and Mark Baker, my beloved
friend and advocate who has always been there. As Mark has said,
"If the rabbi were a paying customer, I'd be able to build half my
practice around him." To these and many other attorneys whose
love of their people impelled them to take out many hours to stand
in court to defend us after countless arrests in acts of nonviolent
civil disobedience, we are forever indebted.

Principles of Spiritual Activism is a compilation of essays, many
of which first appeared in a wide variety of newspapers and journals over the years. I am deeply grateful to those editors who
opened their pages to me: Rabbi Shalom Klass and Rabbi Jerry
Greenwald of *The Jewish Press*, Rabbi Bruce Warschal and Andy
Polin of The Miami Jewish Journal, and many others. Bruce and
Andy deserve special credit as their views differ dramatically from
mine; not once, however, were any of my essays turned down
when our opinions diverged. The same unfortunately, cannot be
said of some newspapers sponsored by Jewish Federations. For
years I have publicly maintained that Federation papers are less
able to publish essays or opinions that go against the establishment norms of their sponsoring organization.

When the editor of the New York weekly newspaper sponsored by the Jewish Federation read this assertion, he invited me to
write a monthly column, an offer I happily accepted. In time, however, it became clear that my claim had been correct. An essay I
wrote entitled "There Must Be Ethics in Accepting Money for
Activism," which is included in this selection, was held back for
years. Other essays published here that deal with such establishment organizations as the Conference of Presidents of Major
American Jewish Organizations and the United States Holocaust
Memorial Museum, were rejected although they were published in
other papers around the country. Believing that a regular colum-

nist should have the right to express his or her opinion without veto, I stopped my monthly column. Even so, I am grateful for the period during which my articles found a home there and wish to acknowledge here that the idea of compiling this book originated when some of my essays were first published in that newspaper.

I am also indebted to Bernard Scharfstein, publisher of KTAV, for encouraging me to compile these essays into a single volume. Over the years Bernie has been a wonderful friend. I am grateful for his guidance, supreme patience and personal concern.

This collection also includes references to several individuals of whom I am critical, some of them people who have devoted years of service to our people. As I have grown older, I have come to learn how to compartmentalize, how to distinguish between the individual and the issue in which we are in disagreement. Indeed, while disagreeing with these individuals on particular issues, I thank them for all the good they have done for *Am Yisrael*.

There is no rabbi who is as blessed as I am with a synagogue as supportive as mine, the Hebrew Institute of Riverdale. It has been my honor to serve as its spiritual leader. My deepest gratitude is owed to its leadership, Stanley Langer, Hillel Jaffe, Bernie Horowitz, David Eiseman, Howard Jonas, Steven Pretsfelder, Lewis Bernstein, Ari Hait, Ronnie Becher, Dr. Jeffrey Gurock and to our first president, David Mann, whose vision has made it possible for our synagogue to grow and flourish. Sharona Margolin Halickman serves as religious mentor of our synagogue, embodying some of the most important elements of spiritual activism. Linda Basch and her staff, who perform great acts of spiritual activism by reaching out regularly to Seniors, some confined to their homes, and to hundreds of our "Special Friends," those in our community who are developmentally challenged, deserve special recognition and gratitude. Sue Prince, my loyal assistant over many years, Ruth Balter of blessed memory, and more recently, Beverly Muller, Anita Nerwen and Sandy Weitz, have all stood faithfully at my side, truly my staff and support. Special appreciation also goes to Shimmie Kaminetsky, the Executive Director of our synagogue; talented, a mensch par excellance, there is only one indispensable Shimmie.

My rabbinic colleagues at the Hebrew Institute with whom I have been associated over the years have also earned, in addition to my gratitude, my profound admiration and respect: Rabbi Ronald Schwarzberg, Rabbi Chaim Marder, Rabbi Yosef Kanefsky, Rabbi Barry Gelman, Rabbi Aaron Frank, Rabbi David Kalb, Rabbi Shmuel Herzfeld, Rabbi Adam Starr, Rabbi Yamin Levy, Rabbi Ian Pear, Rabbi Yair Silverman and Rabbi Chaim Motzen. My deepest thanks also to Rabbi Dov Linzer, Rosh Ha-Yeshiva of our new rabbinical school, and, of course, to *yedid nafshi*, Dr. Elli Kranzler, whose song and spiritual depth are an essential source of peace and harmony in my life.

I am blessed with a special relationship with my siblings and their families: my sister, Tova Reich, one of the great influences on my life; my brother, my teacher of family values, Rabbi Mordechai Weiss; my sister, my spiritual inspiration, Sara Tov; and my brother, my guide of integrity whom I admire and look up to, Rabbi Dr. David Weiss. Even as we have each taken different paths in life, our love for each other remains deep and abiding, and to each I can only say thank you.

I am also blessed with an enormously patient, forgiving, and good-humored wife, Toby Hilsenrad Weiss, whose understanding and willingness to allow me to stand up for what I believe have earned her my love and deepest gratitude. And, of course, both Toby and I thank God every day of our lives for the blessing of our children, our teachers who have shown us the way: Dena and Mark Levie and their children, Ariella, Shira and Tali; Elana and Michael Fischberger and their children Gilad, Eitan, Rami and Ayelet; and our son, Rabbi Dov Weiss who has been the inspiring force for many of my undertakings and projects.

My mother, Miriam Borenstein Weiss, z'l, from far away is still tapping me on the shoulder showing me the way. My father, Rabbi Dr. Moshe Weiss, to whom this book is dedicated, has taught me to stand up for my beliefs, no matter how unpopular. No words can express the debt I owe to them.